P9-CQN-661

GIN

THE MANUAL

GIN

THE MANUAL

DAVE BROOM

MITCHELL BEAZLEY

TO MY WIFE, PARTNER, AND FRIEND JO.

An Hachette UK Company
www.hachette.co.uk

First published in Great Britain in 2015
by Mitchell Beazley, an imprint of Octopus
Publishing Group Ltd, Carmelite House,
50 Victoria Embankment, London EC4Y 0DZ
www.octopusbooks.co.uk
www.octopusbooksusa.com

Distributed in the US by Hachette Book Group,
1290 Avenue of the Americas, 4th and 5th
Floors, New York, NY 10020

Distributed in Canada by Canadian Manda
Group, 664 Annette St., Toronto, Ontario,
Canada M6S 2C8

ISBN: 978-1-84533-938-8

A CIP record for this book is available from the British Library.

Printed and bound in China.

10 9 8 7 6 5 4 3 2 1

Senior Editor Leanne Bryan
Copy Editor Jo Richardson
Proofreader Constance Novis
Indexer Cathy Heath
Creative Director Jonathan Christie
Art Director Juliette Norsworthy
Designer Geoff Fennell
Picture Research Manager Giulia Hetherington
Production Controller Allison Gonsalves

CONTENTS

INTRODUCTION

My father, he drank whisky; my mother, she drank gin. This may sound like the start of a country and western song, but it was, kind of, the truth – the first bit anyway. My mother didn't really drink; a small sherry before dinner perhaps. Once, however, she did confess to me that "the drink I love the most is a gin and tonic, but, you know..." The sentence didn't need to be finished. Women didn't drink gin. Its taste may have been wonderful, but people would have tutted.

Strangely, though, gin was behind her getting married. Her first date with my father was also the first time she had ever been to a pub. When my dad asked her what she would like to drink, she panicked and said, "Gin and It". She had heard about it, maybe seen it mentioned in a movie, but had never tried it. My mother's first drink was the British equivalent of the Martinez, served in a pub in Glasgow's East End. That gives me a certain sense of pride. The fact that they married soon after and a couple of years later I came along also means that, in some curious way, I have gin to thank for my existence.

Her relationship with gin was a throwback to the gin-fuelled mayhem of London in the eighteenth century; it also carries the chill of Scottish Presbyterian disapproval (and, trust me, there is nothing as fearsome) and the disreputable whiff of the excesses of the Bright Young Things in the twenties and thirties. Gin was flash, too strong, and uncouth. Being assailed by all sides simultaneously has long been part of gin's burden.

My own love of gin began later. In the Scotland where I grew up, men drank whisky. Gin was also seen as an "English" drink, one for snooty golf clubs and a certain social class; a signifier of status, class, and attitude. This was, of course, in the days of gin's decline.

Years on, I had my first Martini. It was made for me by Desmond Payne at the Beefeater distillery, in those days a lonely, echoing place that seemed only to be kept warm by one man's passion. I inhaled the scents of the botanicals, marvelled at the stills, nosed the new make, sipped the drink, and thought, "Where have you been all my life?".

Gin was still in the doldrums. Distillers were flailing around, lowering strength and adding flavours. Then along came Bombay Sapphire and people began to become interested in gin once more. Equally significantly, it coincided with the London cocktail revival, when people of my age could drink classics; a small band of sisters and brothers in the wasteland crying, "We love gin".

Soon after, Charles Rolls flew me to Plymouth in a two-seater plane with two cases of gin in the back (quite why we were taking gin to the distillery I never quite worked out). What followed was the realization that every person worth talking to in Scotch whisky had gin as their first drink. I became a confirmed gin drinker, fascinated by its complexities, revelling in its history, loving its underdog status.

Now, at a time when 20 new brands seem to appear every week and new distilleries are on every corner, all of that seems like a weird dream. Was there really a time when gin wasn't loved, when it was stigmatized, when Martinis were vodka drinks and bartenders thought Negroni was an imported beer? Was there a time when saying you would like to write a gin book would see the publisher politely changing the subject?

Here's to the new world of gin!

HISTORY

What follows is a tale of depravity and joy, of low-life and sophistication, of creativity and unscrupulousness, of medieval mystics and scientists. Gin's globe-spanning story weaves through medicine, alchemy, politics, the birth of national identity and that of the working class, imperialism, the spice trade, war, disease, Prohibition, frivolous Bright Young Things, and hard-eyed WASP businessmen. Gin's praises have been sung by great writers and musicians, its subtleties created by masterly distillers and given extra dimensions by mixologists. In its time, it has variously been blamed for society's ills and become a symbol of middle-class respectability.

Most of all, gin is resilient. It knows that people will eventually come to their senses and appreciate it for what it has always been – a spirit of extraordinary complexity and depth. Listening to gin's story is to sit at the feet of a war veteran and wonder quite how they survived the fantastical escapades they describe. Survive gin did, and prospered. We are now in gin's second Golden Age. How we got here, however, is quite a yarn. So sit back...

Juniperus communis, the Common Juniper, has been used for thousands of years as a cure for numerous ailments.

THE MIRACLE BERRY

The small conifer emerged tentatively, ally to the heaths, grasses, mosses, and lichens covering and colouring the new landscape that the ice had left after it had gouged and scoured the rocks for millennia. With the ice in retreat, juniper with its black berry-like cones was at the forefront of the recolonization of the land by vegetation, and its pollen remained safely preserved in peat banks for Man to discover several millennia later.

Ancient Remedy

In the early days of human civilization, when people cured themselves with whatever the earth could provide, the "berries" of what came to be scientifically named as *Juniperus communis* were valued for their particular potency. The Ancient Egyptians noted in the Ebers Papyrus (c. 1550 BC), one of the oldest records of medical knowledge, how juniper cured jaundice. For the Ancient Greeks, it was both a performance-enhancing drug and a remedy for colic. The father of medicine, Roman physician Dioscorides (c. AD 40–90) detailed the effective use of juniper berries steeped in wine to combat many chest ailments, and also as an abortifacient. Were they distilled? Perhaps. Dioscorides's "pot-on-pot" distillation method would appear in medical and herbal texts over the subsequent 500 years. Pliny the Elder also praised juniper, mentioning it 22 times in his *Naturalis Historia* (c. AD 77–79), where he writes:

> "The seed... dispels flatulency and sudden chills, stops coughs and brings indurations to a head... and the berries taken in red wine act astringently on the bowels... The seed is diuretic in its effects... either as a dose of four berries in white wine or in the form of a decoction of 20 berries in wine."

Medieval Panacea

By the thirteenth century, this miracle berry was one of a dizzying catalogue of ingredients that alchemists and apothecaries were experimenting with in cities such as Bruges. It was in nearby Damme, 7km (4½ miles) away, between 1266 and 1269 that Jacob van Maerlant wrote (in rhyme) the 13-volume encyclopedia *Der Naturen Bloeme*, itself a translation of Brussels-born Thomas of Cantimpré's 20-volume *Liber de Natura Rerum*. In Chapter 8, van Maerlant advises: "cook [juniper] berries in wine for cramps... cook berries in rainwater for stomach pains". He also describes a method of distilling the wood to make oil, which, along with juniper incense and berries stuffed into masks, led the battle against the onslaught of the Black Death (1346–53).

Hieronymus Brunschwig's treatise on distilling of 1500, the title of which translated into English as *The Vertuose Boke of Distyllacyon*, contained a recipe for "water of genyver berries":

> "In the morning/at nine at night/drink of the same water at each time an ounce/is good against the gravell in the limbs and in the bladder/it causes the urine to come out and well to piss..."

This was the age of the herbals – encyclopedias of plants and their curative properties – and juniper played a prominent role in most of them. The Swiss naturalist Conrad Gesner chose to exemplify the distillation of juniper's fruits in his 1559 herbal entitled *The Treasure of Euonymus*. Gesner's herbal also contained a vast recipe for "a most noble water of vertues worthy to be preferred before silver and gold" and listed juniper among 23 base ingredients, while another recipe that claimed to "restoreth youth" had 44. The other ingredients are familiar to gin lovers: grains of paradise, sage, fennel seeds, nutmeg, pepper, bayberry, fresh herbs, cubeb berries, cardamom, and almond. Three years later, William Turner published his *A New Herball*, the first to focus on English plants, including juniper, which he reported "grows plenteously in Kent... in the bishopric of Durham and Northumberland" and could be used as a diuretic, as well as to keep vipers away. This was followed in 1640 by the last of the great herbals, John Parkinson's *Theatrum Botanicum*, in which he wrote: "No man... can easily set down the virtues of the juniper tree", yet undeterred he goes on to try. Juniper, it would seem, was good for treating everything from nosebleeds to the plague, including convulsions during childbirth and asthma. By then, however, in the Low Countries at least, juniper had another valuable attribute, and one that had an affect on wealth as well as health.

Conrad Gesner's *The Newe Jewell of Health* (1576), shows the master and assistant distilling alcohol, using a primitive form of reflux condenser.

1495 VERBATIM

This extravagant recipe starts by taking 10 quarts of wine (or "mother of wine", possibly lees), thinned with clear water or Hamburg beer "until the water has the thickness of buttermilk". It is then distilled in a two-pot still, the head being affixed and sealed with a mixture of egg yolk and flour. You then take 9 parts of this "burned wine" to 1 part of the following spice mix: 12 nutmegs, ginger, galangal, grains of paradise, clove, cinnamon, and cardamom. After this is distilled, you add 4lb of crushed nutmeg, 2 handfuls of dried sage, 1lb of cloves, and, finally, juniper. In the actual recipe, this is referred to as *gorsbeyn de dameren*, which translates literally as "ashes of frog's bones" or, as Van Schoonenberghe (see right) argues, ground dried juniper [*ghurst*] berries [*beyen*]. This mixture is put into a cloth bag and suspended in the pot, then the mixture is redistilled.

In 2014, at G'Vine's (*see* pp.122–3) Cognac HQ (the original recipe calls for wine from close to Cognac), a team including genever historian Phillip Duff and David Wondrich (*see* p.155) re-created this concoction and named it Verbatim.

The Spirit of the Low Countries

We don't know his name, but we can surmise that a certain merchant who lived between Arnhem and Appeldorn in 1495 was rich, because who else but a wealthy man would have a household book handwritten for his own delight? And who else would have been able to afford the outrageous amount of spices needed to make a recreational spirit, the earliest found to date to use juniper (*see* panel, left)? Those spices would have come to him overland from the East to Constantinople, then Venice. This was a decadent, liquid manifestation of power and also a clear indication that people were drinking for pleasure. Two years later, "brandy" – a catch-all term for spirits at that time – was being taxed in Amsterdam.

Water of Life

To understand gin, you must first understand genever, the rise of which came on the back of warfare, religious persecution, nation building, and trade. Its greatest historian is Dr. Eric Van Schoonenberghe, without whose texts this chapter would have been considerably sketchier. There was a rich seam of alchemical-related writings in Dutch from the thirteenth century onwards, many of which mention juniper. However, it was Johannes de Aeltre's 1351 copy of an earlier tract titled *Aqua vite, dats water des levens of levende water* that is particularly significant in highlighting a shift in the spirit's function. In it, he stated that *aqua vitae*:

> "Het doet oec den mensche droefheit vergeten
> Ende maecten van hertten vro ende oec stout
> ende coene."
> "It makes people forget about sadness,
> and makes their hearts happy and brave."

Clearly, a change had taken place. People were realizing that what had been regarded purely as a medicine had another property. And so juniper berries were ready to assume their modern role.

The position of Bruges as a centre for trade and intellectual investigation dwindled in the fifteenth century when the river Zwin silted up, and the focus shifted 90km (56 miles) east to Antwerp where, in 1552, Philippus Hermanni wrote *Een Constelijck Distileerboec*. It not only featured a recipe for juniper berry water but

Crock bottles, like these antique examples from Dutch distiller Bols, are still used to bottle genever today.

went into forensic detail about how to distil. It would become the manual for distillers in the Low Countries.

All of the healing waters up until this point had been wine-based, but a succession of poor harvests and cold weather prompted distillers to turn to what was around them, initially sour beer and subsequently rye and malted barley. But there was another reason for the shortage of wine. The year 1568 saw the start of the Eighty Years' War between the Low Countries and their then rulers Spain. A Protestant uprising, centred around Antwerp, was violently suppressed by the Spanish. The combination of increased religious persecution and a fall in trade prompted a mass exodus of artisans, distillers, and merchants. Six thousand refugees went to London alone during this period, while others went to the northern Netherlands, Berlin, Cologne, and France. As Antwerp's importance declined, distillers re-established themselves in the towns of the new Dutch Republic, such as Schiedam, close to Rotterdam. Others moved to Amsterdam, Weesp, and Hasselt (now in Belgium), joined by a second wave in 1601 when the rulers of the Spanish-controlled south, Archdukes Albert and Isabella, banned distillation from grains, citing the need for bread, an edict that remained in force for 112 years.

Added Values

Hitherto, the rich had drunk wine and brandy; the poor, beer and malt spirit, but by the start of the seventeenth century, war was imposing a change. In 1606, the Dutch Republic taxed brandy, anise, and genever. Since prior to this only brandy had been taxed, it's evident that genever was now being more widely consumed. This also resulted in a shift in flavour. In order to produce a more refined spirit to appeal to the brandy-deprived merchant class, Dutch distillers began to aromatize their malt wine, primarily with juniper (*jenever*) and other spices that were becoming easier to obtain. In 1602, the Dutch East India Company (*Vereenigde Oostindische Compagnie* or VOC) received its charter. Until its dissolution in 1799, it was the world's most powerful trading body, with a virtual monopoly on the spice trade. The Dutch Golden Age had begun.

Among the refugees from Antwerp were the Bulsius family who, after a short period in Cologne, had arrived in Amsterdam in 1575, changed their name to Bols, and began making liqueurs. By 1664, they had added genever to their range (*see* pp.171–3 and 178). Both styles of drink required exotic ingredients, and the family established close ties with the 17-man Council of the VOC. In 1700, at the height of the VOC's power when it had risen to the status of a *de facto* state, Lucas Bols became a shareholder, allowing him preferential access to the spices as well as a distribution network for his products.

The VOC's nigh-on 5,000-strong fleet made Amsterdam the centre of world trade. As E M Beekman observes in *Fugitive Dreams*, "monopolies can be legislated, but they can only be maintained by force..." Yet what did Amsterdam's merchants and distillers care of the brutalities in the East when its riches were being unloaded on the city's wharves? In came the spices and silks; out went the genever. By this time, the Dutch navy and army were receiving a daily ration of genever. Colonists in the East Indies would have *soopjes* (shots) of "parrot soup", "fathead", and "hopping water" throughout the day, and take their "mosquito net" nightcap before sleep. Genever was also used in bartering. The missionary Herman Neubronner van der Tuuk was offended when a Batak chief in Sumatra asked for 12 bottles of genever in exchange for a sacred text.

The trading post of the Dutch East India Company, the VOC, in the Hooghly district of Bengal, in India. Painting by Hendrik van Schulenburgh, from 1665.

Holland Goes Global

Genever had become part of a complex web of trade and culture, one thread in the intricate tapestry of identity that the new nation was stitching for itself. As it began to be distributed around the world, to western and South Africa, India, Japan, China, the Caribbean, South America, and Europe, it became a signifier for the Dutch. It wasn't just genever, it was "Hollands". Production continued to rise. Grain came in from the Baltic, and malted barley from England. Casks were needed, made by coopers such as Petrus de Kuyper of Horst, whose son Jan opened a distillery in Schiedam in 1752, its smoke and scents mingling with the effusions from the town's other 126 operations.

The creation in 1713 of the Austrian Netherlands (now Belgium) had, finally, seen distilling recommence there, though contemporary reports suggested that quality was not particularly high. By the end of the century there was also an increase of gin (*genièvre*) distilling in France, which, up until then, had banned distillation from grain. Although exports of genever to England were interrupted by four wars between the English and the Dutch (1652–4, 1665–7, 1672–4, and 1780–4), by the end of the eighteenth century, "Hollands" was selling in the London's new "strong water shops" at half the price of French brandy. As the capital's fledgling distillers were struggling to shake off the stigma that had attached itself to gin, genever entered the nineteenth century with confidence. It wasn't only its colonies and neighbours that wanted genever, now America did too.

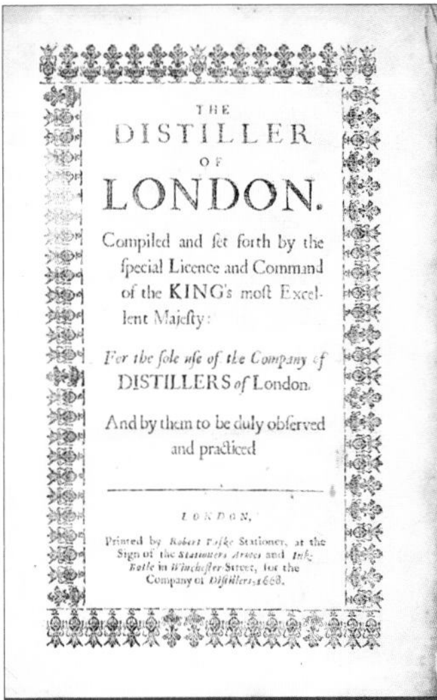

THE
DISTILLER
OF
LONDON.

Compiled and fet forth by the fpecial Licence and Command of the KING's moft Excellent Majefty:

For the fole ufe of the Company of DISTILLERS *of* London.

And by them to be duly obferved and practiced

LONDON,

Printed by *Robert Tafke* Stationer, at the Sign of the *Stationers Armes* and *Ink-Botle* in *Winchefter* Street, for the Company of *Diftillers*, 1668.

MODERN GIN IN THE MAKING

***The Distiller of London* of 1698 contains a number of proto-gin recipes. Most often, the long and complex recipe XXVI is reprinted, but I find XXXIII more intriguing. Juniper is the first ingredient, alongside dried parings of quince and pippin (apple), lemon and orange peel, nutmeg, aniseed, and clove. After distillation, strawberries and raspberries are macerated in the spirit, prior to sweetening. It's as modern as you like.**

The Difficult Birth of British Gin

Although the recipe contained in Sir Hugh Plat's *Delightes for Ladies* is often quoted as the first English juniper-flavoured spirit, it isn't. It does, however, demonstrate how spirits were no longer the preserve of alchemists and apothecaries, and could – indeed should – be made by the lady of a household. Distilling was now practised by scientists and doctors, the gentry, and specialists, many of whom were refugees from the Low Countries. By 1621, there were 200 registered distillers in London, and in 1638, The Worshipful Company of Distillers was granted a Royal Charter and the power

DUTCH COURAGE

Soldiers played a strange role in English gin's story. According to some gin historians, it was thanks to them bringing back "Dutch Courage" from the battlefields of the Netherlands at any point between Elizabethan times (about 1560–1600) and the Thirty Years' War (1618–48) that prompted gin's rise in popularity. However, the idea that the troops were advocates of genever is, I think, over-simplistic. When they returned, unemployed, they were looking for cheap spirits; the fact that by the eighteenth century the cheapest was gin was pure coincidence.

to control the quality of the spirit being made. The 1698 reprint of its recipe book *The Distiller of London* (*see* panel, opposite) instructed "that all wines, low wines, lees of wines, and spirits under proof be first distilled... into strong proof whereby they may be corrected... before they are compounded".

Dutch Influence

Among the influx of immigrants into England was William Y-Worth of Rotterdam, a respected alchemist and confidant of Isaac Newton who, in 1692, published *The Compleat Distiller*. Y-Worth's book is a clear account of the Dutch methods of distilling and compounding. He has some sharp words to say about the "defective" approach of the Worshipful Company, though his only mention of juniper is in the medicinal *Pharmacopoeia Spagyrica* section. Along with improved Dutch distilling techniques, the seventeenth century also saw the importation of genever, both legally and by smugglers, and this was soon regarded as the measure against which British distillers should compare their gins. At this time, members of Scotland's Haig distilling dynasty were also studying genever production in Schiedam (*see* p.20).

By this time, Britain also had a Dutch king, William III, who had been invited to take the throne in 1688. His accession is often cited as the trigger that prompted people to start drinking gin out of patriotic enthusiasm. In reality, the gentry were already drinking it, and its consumption only spread thanks to an act of political expediency. In 1690, Parliament passed "An Act for encouraging the distilling of brandy and spirits from corn". Lowering the duties on spirits made from English corn and initially banning French brandy was a way to curry favour with farmers and landowners who were experiencing a corn surplus. It wasn't an attempt to encourage people to drink gin, though they did, and how. Deregulation of production meant that anyone could now distil or compound. As a result, consumption of spirits rose from 2,600,363 litres (572,000 gallons) in 1684 to 5,455,308 litres (1.2 million gallons) in 1700. The combination of cheap corn from 1715–55 and a mass of new distillers saw prices crash, and as they did, so did quality. By 1720, the Gin Craze had taken hold.

Crazed Times

Out of chaos, in the eighteenth century, Britain formed itself into a new nation, and the greatest manifestation of that bedlam was London. The city was expanding rapidly, with people packed into its growing slums. It was a febrile time, with almost constant war, the continuing threat of Jacobite rebellion, and uncontrolled financial speculation. The siren call of London's possibilities lured ever more souls into its fetid embrace, only to dash them into its gutters. Some, though, prospered and learned a trade, or obtained a position, but the majority salved their misery with the balm provided by Mother Geneva.

By 1720, 90 per cent of English spirits were being distilled in London and most of that was gin. It was cheap, strong, imitated the "Hollands" that the gentry were drinking, and easily available from taverns, public houses, coffee houses, and the grimy gin shops that festooned the city's alleyways. You could buy it from the chandler's shop, where the poor got their twists of sugar, stale bread, and hard cheese, from barrows, or from hawkers. The rise in gin consumption by the lower classes had become enough of an issue for the government to pass an Act in 1729 to try and curb demand. However, it saw

William Hogarth's *Gin Lane*, which was issued in 1751 in support of the Gin Act: accurate depiction or over-heated propaganda?

THE GIN ACTS

1729 A higher duty of 5 shillings per gallon on compound waters. Retail licence now cost £20.

1733 The extra duty on compound spirits scrapped. Street vendors banned. £10 fine to be paid if caught. Informers to be paid £5 on conviction and payment of fine.

1736 £50 licences for selling distilled spirits; duty £1 per gallon. £100 fine for unlicensed retailers. £10 fine for street sales. Illegal to sell less than 2 gallons wholesale.

1743 Duties on low wines doubled to 2 pence per gallon, duty of spirits 6 pence per gallon. Licence cut to £1. Gin to be sold in licensed premises only. Distillers not permitted to retail.

1747 Wholesale distillers allowed to retail on payment of a £5 licence.

1751 Duty rises to one shilling per gallon; cost of licence rises to £2. Distillers banned from retailing. Licensed premises restricted to inns, alehouses, and taverns and gin only for sale to publicans whose premises are rateable at more than £10 *per annum*.

1760 Duty increases of 5 pence on low wines and 1 shilling 3 pence on corn-based spirits. Export subsidies offered.

just 453 of the new licences (costing the equivalent of a year's income) being granted and had no effect on the volume being sold. Distilling and selling was becoming the sole option for earning money in the slums.

The rise in duty not only attempted to raise much-needed revenue (the century's constant wars had to be paid for), but played well with the neo-Prohibitionists. It also cleverly avoided conflict with the vested interests of the distillers and landowners by only targeting the estimated 1,500 compounders. The problem was that it didn't work, and by 1730 gin consumption had reached 13,638,276 litres (3 million gallons). Opposition to gin had become a moral crusade fought with sermons, plays, and pamphlets relating dreadful tales of debauchery, murder, and dissipation.

In 1736, a third Gin Act was passed (*see* panel, left), but in spite of its draconian measures designed to drive gin out, only 20 of the new £50 licences were issued and the demon spirit was even more freely available. Two years later, production topped six million gallons. The fury of gin's opponents was only matched by that of those they were targeting. They queued up in front of "Puss and Mew" devices, pioneered by Dudley Bradstreet, where, by a painted sign of a cat, patrons whispered "Puss". On the affirmative response of "Mew", the patron placed two pennies in the drawer that shot out and were dispensed a dram through a lead pipe under the cat's paw. Informers, eager to claim their rewards, were now organizing themselves into gangs but, if uncloaked, they could pay a very high price. In 1738, for example, the body of a deceased woman informer was dug up and a stake driven through her heart. Drinking gin had now become an act of civil disobedience; the mob was restless. In time, magistrates fearful of attack gave up trying to impose the law.

Out of the eight million gallons of gin produced in 1742 (over two gallons per capita), only 40 gallons of licensed gin were sold. Revenue was now desperately needed to help pay for the 80,000 troops sent to fight in the war of the Austrian Succession (1740–8), so the Government changed tack with yet another Act (*see* panel, left). Initially it appeared to work, with 481,000 of the low-priced licences being taken out between 1743 and 1747. The distillers, however, objected

The perils of gin-drinking among young women was another popular theme for illustrators such as Thomas Rowlandson, who produced this drawing at the beginning of the 1800s.

to not being allowed to sell direct and, in 1748, they and the compounders were once again permitted to retail. At this precise moment, however, the troops returned, prompting a gin-fuelled crime wave.

London was in crisis. The city's birth rate fell between 1720 and 1750, while the death rate rose, with infant mortality averaging 242 deaths per 1,000 deaths *per annum* between 1730 and 1779. Alcoholism played its part, but gin was far from being the sole cause. The Gin Craze was born out of poverty. Although gin consumption began to fall during the late 1740s, the war with gin was soon once again top of the political agenda. In 1751, artist William Hogarth's print of *Gin Lane* (*see* p.16) was issued with its hellish depiction of life in the "rookeries" (slums) around St Giles. It depicts a fractured society, with gin as a symbol of its moral and physical decline. The drunken slatternly mother letting her child tumble to its death in the centre represented not just Mother Genever but women themselves.

From Notoriety to Acceptability

"If a woman accustoms herself to dram-drinking she... becomes the most miserable as well as the most contemptible creature on earth." So wrote the anonymous author of *A dissertation on Mr Hogarth's Six Prints* in 1751. If women are depraved, the abolitionists posed, then what hope has society? Women are meant to hold society together, they argued, not be the ones with bottles in their skirts selling gin at 5am. More to the point, if they are bad mothers, then where is the next lot of cannon fodder coming from? Yet selling gin was one of the few ways that single women could make money. The same year, yet another Gin Act was passed (*see* panel, p.17), which finally appeared to work and, bar for a spike in 1756, consumption continued to fall. Any residual thirst for cheap gin was washed away between 1757–63 when poor harvests meant that no grain was distilled, and small distillers shut up shop. With gin now expensive to make, prices rose and with them quality. The Gin Craze was over and spirits were returned to the hands of the wealthy, the same people who had been drinking rum, brandy, and genever through its duration.

Gin distilleries were now owned by men of considerable substance – families such as Boord,

Currie, and Booth – and in 1769 Alexander Gordon started distilling in Bermondsey, south London (*see* pp.87–8). By the 1780s, James Stein had installed a gin plant at his Kilbagie whisky distillery in Fife, Scotland capable of producing 5,000 gallons of "Hollands" a day, and although his export licence was revoked, it was a sign that London gin distillers no longer had a monopoly. Thomas Dakin had established a gin distillery in Warrington, northwest England, in 1761 (*see* pp.69 and 89), while in 1793 the Coates family started up in Plymouth (*see* p.104). Four large new distilleries in Bristol, a trio in Liverpool, and increased exports of spirit for rectification from Scotland also put pressure on the London firms.

Gin was, tentatively, becoming an acceptable drink, but it was far from the spirit we know today. In his 1757 book *The Complete Distiller*, Ambrose Cooper advised distillers to follow a Dutch method, with the encouragement that if they were "careful in distilling and rectifying [their] malt spirit, may make Geneva equivalent to that of the Dutch". Y-Worth's message still ran true (*see* p.15).

The 1751 Gin Act brought about the death of Madam Genever ... or did it?

MORE TURPENTINE THAN GIN

Ambrose Cooper in *The Complete Distiller* of 1757 differentiates between the "distilled spiritous water of juniper" and "the common sort [which] is not made from juniper berries... but from Oil of Turpentine". He then gives two recipes: one for 1.3kg (3lb) of macerated berries distilled in 45 litres (10 gallons) of spirit and another that adds 50ml (2fl oz) oil of turpentine and 3 handfuls of bay salt to 90 litres (20 gallons) of spirit.

The Rise of the Cocktail

If gin wasn't reaching the audience that its new monied distillers felt it deserved, by the start of the nineteenth century, it was beginning to inch its way across the English social spectrum, even achieving a certain bohemian approval. According to Thomas Medwin, Lord Byron, whom he met in Pisa, Italy, in the 1820s, kept his stamina up by indulging "too freely in wine, and his favourite beverage Hollands, of which he drinks a pint almost every night". Byron teased his guest in return: "...why don't you try it, gin-and-water is the source of all my inspiration". Notably, though, it was still Hollands, not British gin, that was being drunk. The same would have been the case for the gin punch favoured by the members of London's Garrick Club or in the new short drink named after John Collins, the head waiter at Limmer's Old House, a hotel in Conduit Street, Mayfair in the 1830s.

Class Customs

As Olivia Williams recounts in her book *Gin Glorious Gin*, in 1833 the London magazine, *The Spectator*, listed genever and brandy as being a staple of the middle class household's purchases, while "home-made spirits (gin and whisky) are falling on the poor". Hollands was still regarded as superior, and there were further attempts to make it in Britain, with the Haigs trying to market their Scottish-made version in London in 1807. The distiller Robert More, who had trained in Scheidam, was selling "Geneva" produced at his Underwood distillery in Falkirk, Scotland, in 1828, but it wasn't to work, and the next year he was declared bankrupt.

British gin was still a drink of the working classes. In his 1836 essay *The Streets at* Night, Charles Dickens portrays the rowdy post-theatre crowd in London calling for "goes" (drams) of gin and purl - aromatized beer dosed up with gin. Imports still outstripped domestic production and, in addition, there was still considerable smuggling. Carpeau and Stival's Citadelle distillery in Dunkirk, northern France, was given royal dispensation to distil with grain in 1785 with the specific purpose of smuggling it into England, a state of affairs that continued until 1810, even as the Napoleonic Wars were being fought. It was this tale that inspired Alexandre Gabriel to create his Citadelle brand (*see* pp.118 and 158).

The British legislators then came up with a smart idea to boost domestic spirits. In 1825, they slashed duties from 10 shillings 6 pence to 6 shillings. Gin was now cheaper than beer and in a year consumption jumped from 3.7 to 7.4 million gallons. As Samuel Morewood reported in 1838, this did not improve quality. Because of the poor standard of the base spirit, he wrote: "All spirits were obliged to pass through the medium of [the rectifiers] who were then by a mistaken enactment made the arbiters of public taste."

The return of cheap gin also created a new place in which to drink it, the gin palace, which dazzled among London's malodorous thoroughfares. Glass-fronted, brightly lit, with long bars and barrels of gin behind, gin palaces appeared to offer a high-class opportunity to sip elegant drinks. It was a chimera. They were no more than tarted-up gin shops, seatless spaces for the poor to obliterate themselves with low-grade booze once again. Nothing had been solved. As Dickens put it in his essay on gin palaces in 1835, "Gin-drinking is a great vice in England, but poverty is greater." Realizing their mistake, the government removed the duty on beer in 1830, prompting a rush back to pubs, which now took design cues from the gin palaces (with added seats), giving them the look of the Victorian pub seen today. By the end of the 1830s, the era of the gin palace was over.

The 1820s saw a second Gin Craze, this time centred around London's gin palaces, like this one.

New Gin Styles

The gin distillers were, however, organizing themselves. From 1820–40, the Rectifiers Club met monthly, and while the group had a certain whiff of the cartel about it, the Club standardized practices, while also addressing the issue of inferior base spirit. In 1827, Robert Stein installed his new patent continuous still at Kilbagie (*see* p.19), a design then improved by Aeneas Coffey in 1832 (*see* illustration, opposite). The previous year in Warrington (*see* p.19), Mary Dakin bought a Corty rectifying head for her gin still, and in 1836 installed another new rectifying head designed by a Mr Carter (*see* pp.42–3). The result of all of these innovations was a cleaner base spirit, which in turn meant that there was less need to overload it with heavy botanicals. The new clarity allowed a widening of the botanical palette - more citrus, sweet spices, cardamom, caraway, and so on - and, consequently, gins of greater complexity. In London, gin distillers were now grouped together in Bermondsey, Lambeth, and Clerkenwell, where, in 1798, Gordon's had joined Nicholson's and Booth's. By the middle of the century, the Plymouth distillery (*see* p.19) was supplying 1,000 barrels of Navy Strength a year to the Royal Navy.

This period also saw gin being used to dilute medicinal concoctions. The officers in the Navy cut their dose of antimalarial Angostura bitters with Plymouth gin, thereby creating pink gin. In order to prevent scurvy, all vessels had by law to carry limes, which were most easily transportable in the form of the cordial created by Lauchlin Rose in 1862. Thus, taken with gin, a drink named after the surname of the Navy's Surgeon-General, Sir Thomas Gimlette, was invented. Even the Army got in on the act, offsetting the bitterness of antimalarial tonic waters by mixing them with gin.

The publishing in Britain of William Terrington's *Cooling Cups and Dainty Drinks* in 1869 also pointed to a further stage in gin's evolution. Gin was becoming respectable and more sophisticated as a drink, since it could now be served cooled by ice, which was more widely available. Gin cups, such as the No. 1 famously created by (or for) Mr Pimm's oyster warehouse, were gaining in popularity. The clearest indication of what was on offer in the way of gin from public houses is revealed in Loftus's *New Mixing and Reducing Book*

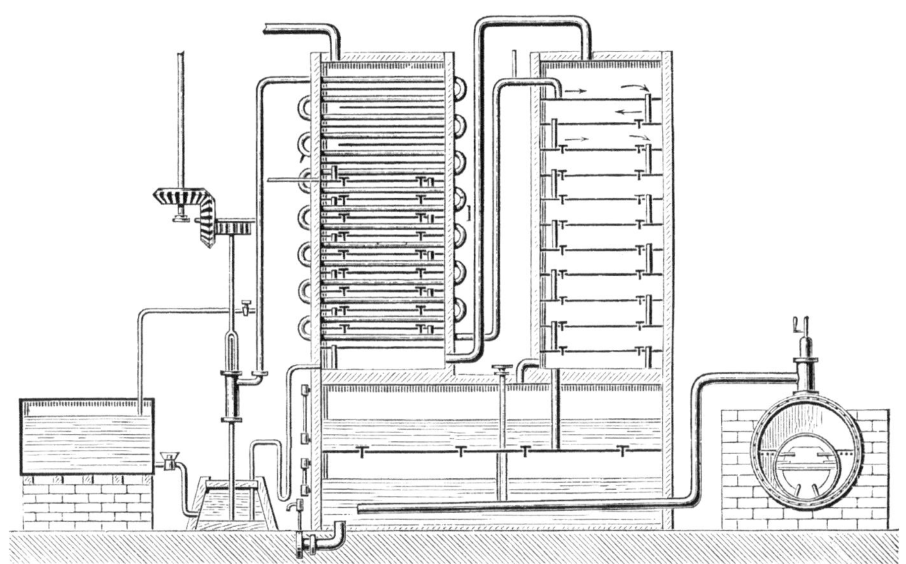

The 1832 invention of the Coffey still by Irishman Aeneas Coffey led to an improvement in the quality of gin.

of 1869, where we learn that it would either come from the rectifier ready sweetened or be adjusted in the pub. Each brand had also established its own style: "Hodges, Booth's, Vicker's, and Nicholson's... have each their characteristic flavour... while the differences between Liverpool and Bristol... or Bristol and Plymouth is as remarkable as the difference... between Scotch and Irish malt whiskey." Loftus even offered guidance on how to give English gin "the creaminess and smoothness much admired in Geneva... mostly the result of age" by adding sugar, garlic, or sliced horseradish! He also observed the general shift in gin style preference: "Strong or unsweetened gin is in comparatively little request... and only amongst the respectable or monied classes." The majority of people were now drinking Old Tom, the sweetened gin named either after a cat that fell in a vat, or more likely after "Old" Thomas Chamberlain of Hodge's distillery. Consumption was, however, restricted to England. Export only started in any significant volume from 1850, when Sir Felix Booth successfully lobbied for excise duties on export gin to be dropped. After that, London's gins headed mainly to the Empire market.

In the 1870s, phylloxera (the blight that devastated the great French vineyards in the late nineteenth century) removed Cognac from menus, allowing gin (and whisky) to become the spirit of choice for the middle class, evidenced by the appearance of gin drinks, such as the punch, julep, cocktail sling, and sangaree in 1871's *The Gentleman's Table Guide*. By then, the old distillers had been joined by Charles Tanqueray, who started compounding in 1830 (*see* pp.110–2), Walter and Alfred Gilbey, and James Burrough who, in 1863, bought John Taylor's gin distillery in Cale Street, Chelsea. In 1876, his Beefeater dry gin (*see* p.63) was launched to tap into the demand among gin's new consumers for an unsweetened style akin to the then new "dry" Champagnes. English distillers now looked west to America, another market that was opening up, and one that had long developed a taste for gin.

Madam Genever's Reign

The nineteenth century was to be genever's golden age. The little town of Schiedam, close to Rotterdam, had a scant 37 distilleries in 1700, but a hundred years later there were 250, and by the 1880s they numbered 392. The industry was no longer solely supplying the domestic market: 80 per cent of Schiedam's genever headed out of its port where it joined brands such as Amsterdam's Bols (*see* p.12 and p.13) being shipped to Africa, Europe, southeast Asia, and America. Malt wine

Schiedam became the capital of Dutch gin distilling in the nineteenth century.

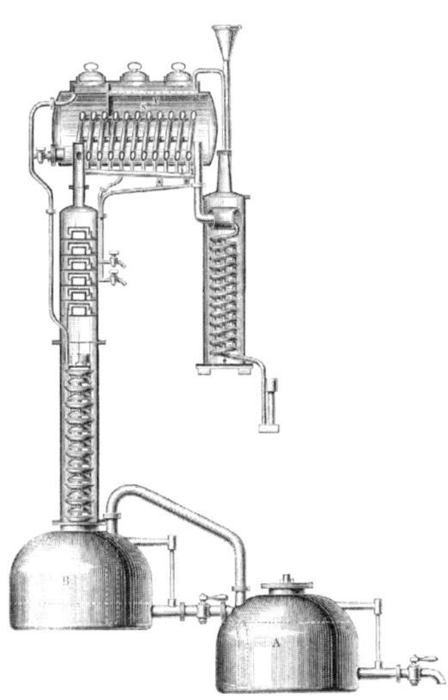

Belgian distillers adopted the Cellier Blumenthal still design in the 1820s.

was also being exported as a base spirit to distillers in England, France, and Germany.

Everything from malting to bottling took place in the town. The soot from Scheidam's hundreds of distillery chimneys mingled with that from the kilns of its 62 malt houses. The blackened air, fanned lightly by the sails of the town's 15 windmills, earned the city the name "Black Nazareth". The boom was not to last. Schiedam's importance started to decline in the late 1880s as the country's larger firms turned their back on malt wine (the town's speciality) in preference of the cheaper base spirit industrially produced from sugar beet. This change mirrored what had already taken place in Belgium. In the 1820s, Belgian distillers were quick to install Brussels-based Cellier Blumenthal's column stills (*see* left), while Belgium's independence in 1830 saw a drop in taxes, a ban on Dutch genever, and a doubling in the number of distilleries to 1,092 with exports starting to Brazil, Africa, India, New Zealand, Australia, and China. Consolidation soon followed, with the bulk being made by large urban distilleries using sugar beet base spirit. This new (*jonge*), light genever became a low-price working class drink, prompting Belgium's very own Gin Craze, whose opponents countered the rise in consumption with messages and images eerily reminiscent of those used in London a century before. Madam Genever was not dead.

America's Gift to the Globe

Gin became a world spirit thanks to America, but America's taste for gin didn't start with London gins. For much of the nineteenth century, when Americans drank gin they drank genever, which had been exported to the continent since at least 1732, with Bols starting to ship in 1750 (*see* p.12 and p.13). Even by the end of the century, genever was being imported in vastly larger quantities than that from Britain, and it's genever (and, in time, Old Tom) that provided the foundation for America's first popular gin drinks and cocktails. As Lesley Solmonson points out in *Gin: A Global History*, it was Hollands that put Rip Van Winkle to sleep for 20 years.

When American distillers began making their own gin, it was to a genever recipe – and it was aged. Samuel McHarry in his 1809's *The Practical Distiller* (*see also* p.181) gives a recipe for gin made with clarified whiskey and an equal quantity of water "together with a sufficient quantity of juniper berries, a handful of hops [plus isinglass, lime water, and salt]." This gin, he adds, "...when fined, and two years old, will be equal, if not superior to Holland gin".

It's this recipe that Brooklyn-based New York Distilling Company has re-created for its Chief Gowanus (*see* p.181), and appropriately, too. Brooklyn was a hub of early distilling and is where, in 1808, Hezekiah Pierrepont founded the Anchor Distillery, said to be the first commercial gin plant in the USA. According to Henry Reed Stiles's *A History of the City of Brooklyn*, Anchor "kept the gin for a full year after it was made by which it acquired the mellowness for which it was peculiarly esteemed". Of the spirits distilled in South Brooklyn's six distilleries in 1851, 2.9 million gallons of whiskey were rectified, much of it into gin.

America made gin because America began drinking mixed drinks. What started as simple, single-serve punches (slings) became fixes, sours, daisies, juleps, and smashes, and, with the addition of bitters at the start of the nineteenth century, "bittered slings" or "cocktails". These were short, preferably cold, drinks to be taken quickly, as eye-openers, hangover cures, or apéritifs, and all could be made with genever. Initially, they were all morning drinks. The wider availability of ice from 1830 onwards made the drinks colder, as did the advent of the cocktail shaker in the late 1840s. As the drinks changed, so did their surroundings. Saloons were now, as Solmonson argues, designed to lure people in and keep them drinking.

While less scabrous than Hogarth (*see* p.16), the Temperance movement also played the "family values" card heavily.

With the saloons came bartenders and with bartenders came showmanship. The first great bartending superstar, Jerry Thomas, started mixing in 1849, and by 1862 had written the first cocktail book. By then, Thomas and his colleagues had "improved" the simple gin drinks. In came apricot brandy, absinthe, Chartreuse, and other ingredients, but the most significant shift took place when vermouth was found to be the Romeo to gin's Juliet. The gin Manhattan, aka the Turf Club, emerged in the 1880s. Its first written reference is in 1884, though Terrington (*see* p.22) has a remarkably similar-sounding mix – alongside the vermouth-heavy Martinez. Both were either Hollands-

or Old Tom-based. Of dry gin there is no trace. Harry Johnson's 1888 *Bartenders' Manual* has 11 gin drinks with Hollands, eight with Old Tom; Jerry Thomas's 1888 edition is 6:4 in favour of Hollands; and "The Only William" Schmidt's *The Flowing Bowl* of 1892 is 11:5 in favour of Hollands. By 1908, however, William "Cocktail" Boothby lists six dry gin drinks in his *The World's Drinks and How to Mix Them*, nine each with the two older styles of gin. The tide was turning. America's taste was moving in the dry direction just as it was also going dry.

Gin's Rise, Fall, and Rise

You might think that Prohibition in the USA (1920–33) would have set gin's global aspirations back a generation. Instead, it was the making of the spirit. British distillers, unwilling to abandon their new main market, simply shipped their gin to Canada or the Bahamas from where it flowed steadily into the speakeasies. Yet, while Prohibition didn't *see* the volume of alcohol consumed rise, there was a shift away from beer to spirits. This was when gin first became truly popular.

Bathtub Gin

As William Grimes outlines in his history of the American cocktail *Straight Up or On the Rocks*, drinks also became

Despite the US authorities' best efforts, gin's popularity rose during Prohibition.

pricier. Prior to Prohibition, a cocktail would set you back 20 cents. That price now doubled for a shot at a speakeasy, and would hit $3 at a top-end club. This provided a further incentive to mix drinks at home and impress your friends with your Martini-making skills. After all, as far back as 1894 the tagline for Heublein's pre-mixed gin drinks promoted them as "a better cocktail at home than is served over any bar in the world".

For those who couldn't afford bootlegged imported gin, there was an alternative, rustled up by mixing industrial alcohol and turpentine in a bathtub, its rank taste masked in the glass by creams and sweeteners. Adulterated "gin", an increase in drinking among women, a rise in spirits consumption – sound familiar? Yes, Prohibition was America's very own Gin Craze.

Amazingly, bathtub gin didn't damage the category's image. In fact, gin prospered after 1933. The following year, Gordon's began distilling in the USA. Gilbey followed in 1938, while Canadian distiller, Seagram, began making its eponymous gin in 1939.

Mixed Fortunes

Meanwhile, things were tougher in the Low Countries. In Belgium, in 1919, duties rose fourfold, retail sales were restricted to a minimum of two litres, and spirits were banned in bars in an attempt to curb excessive consumption (this latter restriction would remain in place until 1985). In the Netherlands, the consequences of a refusal to modernize resulted in only 14 distilleries surviving in Schiedam in 1920, and a less nimble negotiation of Prohibition than that accomplished by the British distillers led to sales to the USA dropping off. Add to that the effects of the Great Depression and World War Two, and genever entered the 1950s severely bloodied.

Gin distilleries in the UK, however, prospered. Prohibition increased the number of rich Americans in Europe and, equally significantly, the number of US-trained bartenders, notably Harry Craddock at The Savoy Hotel (*see* p.200) and Harry MacElhone (*see* p.204 and p.208), who began his European career at the New York Bar in Paris that would later bear his name. Europe was now finally up to speed with cocktails, though their consumption was less egalitarian than

A master at work: Harry Craddock brought American-style gin cocktails to London's Savoy Hotel.

in the USA. In London, cocktail drinking was the preserve of the Bright Young Things at their new-fangled "cocktail parties" or flitting around bars like Ciro's, The Savoy, and the Café Royal. Englishmen abroad could sip their Straits Slings in Singapore or the Pegu Club in Rangoon (*see* p.206). Less affluent drinkers could try to emulate the experience with Gordon's ready-to-serve cocktail packs (complete with shaker) or Beefeater's pre-mix range, or just ask for gin and a simple mixer: orange squash, ginger beer, sweet vermouth, tonic, or Dubonnet.

Post-war Trends

Post-Prohibition America had begun to prefer drier drinks both in terms of the type of gin and the style of drink. The flamboyant, sweet, and creamy drinks of the nineteenth century and Prohibition era had gone and with them Hollands and Old Tom, while consumption of dry gin was steadily on the up. Enter the glory years of the Dry Martini, ever increasing in dryness and the quantity consumed: three at lunch, then more at home or in the bar. The pace of 1950s America was brisk and the mood steely in its intent; the Martini perfectly

American-style genever is once again being made in Brooklyn.

fitted the bill. In Britain, on the other hand, most people drank gin with tonic water (conversely a swanky drink in America), or as a Gin and It – the pub version of the Martinez. It was the drink my mother ordered on her first date with my father. She hadn't a clue what it was, but she knew it carried an air of sophistication.

However, a flavourless assassin was preparing to strike. By 1954, one million cases of vodka were being sold every year in the USA, marketed with the boast that it could replace gin in any drink and leave your breath untainted. By 1967, it was outselling gin. If gin was on the slide in the USA, in Britain it had become irredeemably conservative, a drink consigned to golf clubs and yachts (the new "gin palaces"). In short, it was the antithesis of swinging London. Things were hardly any better in The Netherlands. Duties had been eased post-war in order to rebuild the country, with a detrimental effect on distillers who, by the 1970s had embarked on a suicidal price war that commoditized genever and shattered its image. To most drinkers genever wasn't only cheap and old-fashioned, it was almost the same flavour-wise as vodka. The "*jonge*" neutral style had won but it was a Pyrrhic victory.

Gin's Renaissance

The blue bottle came as a surprise to everyone. What was Sidney Frank thinking? Not just gin, but *premium gin*? In 1987, however, that bold move brought a new generation to gin. Bombay Sapphire (*see* pp.70–1) was light, aromatic, and sexy; it revitalized the whole category. Plymouth's regeneration from 1997 by Charles Rolls (now at Fever-Tree) built on this turnaround (*see* p.104). Suddenly distillers like Desmond Payne at Beefeater (*see* p.64) who had kept the gin pennant flying in a sea of vodka were rightly lauded. Gin drinks were now being made again in London and New York. People were looking for sophistication, for classicism. Vodka couldn't deliver that. Gin could.

It took a little longer for genever to catch up, but in recent years a revival – led initially by Bols (*see* pp.171–3 and 178) and its close connections with the world's bartending community – has seen it being taken seriously once more. New gins began to appear almost daily as a consequence of the rise in small-scale distilling, initially in the USA. For decades, American-made gin had been low-priced because gin was, after all, almost dead. The new small-scale distillers saw an opportunity to do for gin what the microbrewery movement had done for beer, namely making it local, premium, feather-ruffling, and historically obsessed yet forward-thinking.

Gins are now made in pretty much every style – ultra-traditional, terroir, genever, cask-rested, Old Tom, or using a "democratic" botanical mix that scales back juniper. Britain has also experienced a juniper-scented explosion of new gin brands – many made at Thames Distillers (*see* p.79) or Langley (*see* p.75) – with a growing number of distilleries following the path created by the first of their number, Sipsmith (*see* pp.107–8).

Gins are now being crafted globally with a new awareness of the local, such as the Cape fynbos used in South Africa's Inverroche (*see* p.125), Australian botanicals in West Winds (*see* p.135), Islay botanicals in The Botanist (*see* p.73), and the mix of exotic and Black Forest-sourced ingredients in Monkey 47 (*see* p.130), whose vastly complex recipe chimes uncannily with those early and lengthy expositions in medieval herbals. In going forwards, gin has come full circle.

Genever is back: Dutch brand Bols has aligned itself closely to the bar community.

PRODUCTION

One thing that has intrigued me for some while isn't so much the fact that there are so many new gins on the market but that new distillers seem to think gin is easy to make. There is more to gin than just bunging some nicely smelling ingredients together and then distilling them. In fact, the more you examine gin, the more head-scratchingly complex the whole affair becomes.

You have to consider the quality of the base spirit and be aware of the shape and size of the still, the speed at which you run it, and when you stop capturing the gin. In addition, you are always thinking in terms of aroma – what does each botanical smell like, does it add texture, where does it emerge on the nose and palate, and then how does it interact when placed alongside others? How also do you ensure consistency between batches if your (natural) ingredients are changing?

When I asked Plymouth Gin's Sean Harrison about all of this, he recommended that I read two books: one on aromatherapy, the other on perfumery. They taught me a huge amount, but they didn't reveal gin's soul. A gin distiller sits at the crossroads of chemistry and artistry.

What follows isn't a guide on how to make gin at home (leave it to the experts, say I), but it might just give you an idea of how complex the whole process is.

Gin's flavour comes from the distillation of natural essential oils.

> "[Organic chemistry] is the chemistry of life itself and of the products of living things... [its] practical application to human need is one of the irreplaceable foundations of modern civilization."
> *An Introduction to Perfumery* by Tony Curtis and David Williams

ESSENTIAL OILS

Gin flavours come from the essential oils within its botanicals (*see* pp.34–7). The closer you look at the properties of these, the more marvellously weird the whole thing becomes.

Juniper, for example, gets its identity from the combination of a small number of major constituent parts, and a large number of smaller ones. Even trace elements at parts per trillion contribute to its overall effect. Juniper has elements of citrus and rose, as well as pine and camphor. This range is similar for each botanical. Even lemon peel smells of orange.

During distillation these aromas vaporize, mingling with those from the alcohol, rising up the still in a supercharged aromatic steam. Each of the different elements within them is then released at a different point. What is happening is a bit like a maniac driving a horse-drawn carriage over a rocky road: eventually the structure gives way and it flies apart. In botanicals, the most volatile (the lightest) are liberated first, with the heaviest only managing to struggle free later on. At the same time, these elements are bonding with similar components from other botanicals, holding hands as they fly upwards. Together, they build complexity.

BOTANICALS

Juniper (*Juniperus communis*)
This, the only essential botanical in gin, grows across Europe, Asia, and North America, with Tuscany and Macedonia being the main areas of production. It is also sourced from Serbia, Bulgaria, and Scandinavia.

Differences in vintage and terroir impact on the aroma of the "berries" (actually soft-scaled cones containing oil-rich seeds), meaning that distillers need to monitor the quality and character of their juniper closely to ensure consistency of aroma. With an easily identifiable central aroma of a heavily scented pine forest (given by alpha-pinene), juniper's aromatic fingerprint spreads much wider into citrus, lavender, camphor, turpentine, green florals, heather, fruit, and resin, an all-pervasive quality that sustains across the length of a gin's delivery.

Understanding juniper gives an insight into how a botanical recipe is put together by accords, supports, and counterpoints. Everything refers back to it. Without juniper, a gin's centre cannot hold and anarchy is loosed upon the spirit.

Coriander Seeds (*Coriandrum sativum*)

The Robin to juniper's Batman, coriander seeds come from a wide area stretching from Morocco, via Romania and Moldova, and into Russia and India. The last produces the most peppery in character, Morocco the most fragrant.

Linalool is the compound that gives coriander seeds their citric edge, which drifts towards lemon grass. Underneath are ginger, thyme, a floral hint (sharing geraniol with juniper), balsam, and a hint of musky earth. From that, you can see how coriander seeds link with juniper as well as adding top notes to the aroma.

A huge range of botanicals can be – and are – used in the making of gin.

Coriander seeds – juniper's trusty sidekick.

Angelica (*Angelica archangelica*)

A member of the carrot family, angelica is grown commercially in Saxony and Flanders. Its dried roots are the most commonly used part of the plant in gin. The initial impression is of a walk in a dry mixed forest, an amalgam of dust, earth, and woodiness. This is a clear demonstration of its usefulness as a base note, its larger molecules holding onto the more excitable volatile ones, balancing and integrating more perfumed elements, as well as adding dryness.

Angelica has a few tricks up its sleeve, however. Sniff it again and there is also pine, a green herbal note, some sweetness, and the dustiness of sage, giving an overall effect like a shaft of sunlight coming through that green forest. It's a player in a number of other spirits: Chartreuse, Bénédictine, and vermouth, allowing further aromatic bridges to be built in cocktails.

Some distillers also use angelica seeds, which are reminiscent of the oily floral/citric brightness of hops (*see* p.38), with an added underlying celery note.

Orris Root (*Iris pallida*; *Iris germanica*)

The root of the sweet iris, orris is cultivated in Tuscany, Morocco, China, and India. The roots are harvested by hand, dried for up to three years to allow the oils to oxidize, and then pounded into powder. Absolute of orris root (a form of concentrated essential oil) is among the most expensive ingredients in perfumery where, as in gin, it is highly prized less for its aromatic qualities than as a fixative. Orris evaporates slowly, holding onto and bonding with volatile elements. Without the right amount of orris and/or angelica, a gin's (or a perfume's) aroma will fly off. It does, however, have a gentle aromatic role that pokes out quietly, late on the palate, adding violet, (think Parma violets), sweet hay, and dry earth.

Citrus (*Citrus*)

Everyone knows the fresh, sharp, sweet zing of citrus. It wakes up the nostrils, gives energy, and lets the sunshine in. These are the same qualities that make it such an important element in gin. Prior to its widespread use, gin's top notes would have been provided by coriander and juniper's upper range.

Lemon and other citrus peels add aromatic lift to gin.

A wide range of citrus peels (occasionally whole fruit) is used, with lemon and orange the most common. These are commonly sourced from southern Spain.

Lemon (*Citrus limon*) adds its intense, clean, sharp, sherbet-like zing (that's citral, by the way) with immediacy. Volatile lemon comes in quickly and leaves almost as fast.

Bitter orange (*Citrus aurantium*) gives an intense, slightly bitter edge, which adds boldness and lift to a gin's mid-palate.

Sweet orange (*Citrus sinensis*) is used, most famously, by Plymouth (*see* p.104) to provide sweet zestiness (unsurprisingly, given the name) and length to the palate.

More recently, **grapefruit** (ultra-fresh and sweet), **pomelo** ("greener" and milder than grapefruit), **bergamot** (highly intense sour-sweet with floral links to coriander), **yuzu** (massively intense fragrance), and **lime** have been used. Lime is also chemically linked to juniper, which could explain why it works so well in G&T.

Liquorice Root (*Glycyrrhiza glabra*)

Ground dried liquorice root, mostly sourced from Indo-China, is another of gin's back-room workers. Its main aromatic compound is anethole (*see* Aniseed, opposite), but gin distillers use it for its glycyrrhizic acid, the compound that carries its sweetness. Since liquorice is 50 times as sweet as sucrose, and sugar doesn't distil over, this is what gives gin its sweetness as well as mouthfeel, softening the drier botanicals and adding texture. Here, then, is the harmony.

Cassia Bark (*Cinnamomum aromaticum*)

The bark of a tree that grows in Vietnam, China, and Madagascar, cassia combines spice with a powerful, slightly dry pungency that has a resinous/medicinal edge. **Sri Lankan cinnamon (*Cinnamomum verum*)** with its warmth and sweetness is more immediately identifiable. Both come across in the middle of the aroma and help to boost floral notes.

Almond (*Prunus dulcis*)

Gin distillers use two types of almond. The more traditional is **bitter almond (var. *amara*)**, which provides a distinctive marzipan note along with subtle nuttiness and a little cherry. **Sweet almond (var. *dulcis*)** gives a honeyed note, helping to add softness to the mouthfeel. Almonds are grown and harvested in the Mediterranean, North Africa, and California.

Spices

Aniseed (*Pimpinella anisum*)

It's the compound anethole that gives aniseed its distinctive "liquorice" taste (though weirdly liquorice doesn't taste of it as strongly). Similarly aromatically related are **fennel seeds (*Foeniculum vulgare*)**, which contribute more of a lemon top note. Some gin distillers also use the warm, pungent **star anise (*Illicium verum*)**.

Cardamom (*Elettaria cardamomum*)

The two main sources of green cardamom's highly aromatic seeds are Mysore and Malabar in India. The latter adds a eucalyptus, almost menthol-like note, while cardamom from Mysore gives more of a warming, aromatic, citric-floral note thanks to our friend linalool. Here is another botanical that both links and extends, though it needs to be used sparingly. **Black cardamom (*Amomum subulatum*)**, which has a deeper and smokier aroma, is less commonly used to flavour gin.

The cardamom pods used to flavour gin are harvested by hand in India.

Cubeb Berries (*Piper cubeba*)

A member of the pepper family (genus **Piper**), cubeb grows in Java. The berries carry the same pungent heat as black pepper, but with more of a high floral tone, a hint of rose (from geraniol), some citrus, and a decided palate heat. There is also some pine here, making them a perfect accord while adding pep to the palate.

Ginger (*Zingiber officinale*)

With its familiar and bold aroma, ginger adds lift and dryness, and carries aromas to the back of the palate.

Grains of Paradise (*Aframomum melegueta*)

Native to western Africa, grains of paradise come from a member of the ginger family. Aromatically, they help to boost coriander's citric-spicy elements, while sharing a similar menthol-citrus warmth with cardamom. There is even a note of lavender, which nods towards juniper.

Flowers such as elderflower are becoming popular botanical ingredients.

Nutmeg (*Myristica fragrans*)
An immediately identifiable warm spice, nutmeg contains pinene in its chemical make-up, and also links into cardamom and cassia.

Herbs and Flowers

Bay (laurel) (*Laurus nobilis*)
This common kitchen herb is beginning to appear in American gins. It has a green pungency, with a light pine note and clove that nudges into eucalyptus, and links well with juniper's more resinous elements.

Chamomile (*Anthemis nobilis*)
Chamomile is becoming widely used in the floral gins, helping to further widen the category's aromatic range. The flowers, dried, give a haunting, heavy top note of sweet hay, apple, and a drowsy summer afternoon.

Elderflower/berry (*Sambucus nigra*)
Another floral that is becoming increasingly popular, the dried flowers of the elder add a honeyed element to gin. The berries are also being used in American gins.

Geranium (*Pelargonium*)
The leaves of geraniums have been widely used in perfume and drinks for centuries. Punchbowls were lined with them to add their scent to the compound. Aromas range from pineapple, through lemon and mint, to the familiar green rose provided by geraniol, which is also present in many other gin botanicals including juniper. Geranium contributes middle notes.

Hops (*Humulus lupulus*)
In old genever recipes, it was the aroma of hops that added lift. There are 120 varieties of this flowering plant, with aromas ranging from citrus to fruit, grass, and pine. Hops provide top notes.

Meadowsweet (*Filipendula ulmaria*)
Gentle but penetrating, with a little almond and occasionally a hint of wintergreen, this perennial herb's own top note is like a mixture of hot butter and honey.

LEGAL DEFINITIONS

Gin must be made from ethyl alcohol flavoured with juniper berries and other botanicals. The predominant flavour must be juniper, and it must be bottled at no less than 37.5% ABV.

Gin
Made by adding natural or approved artificial flavourings to alcohol. No restrictions on colouring or sweetening.

Distilled gin
Made by redistilling neutral alcohol with approved natural or artificial flavourings. After distillation, more ethyl alcohol of the same composition may be added. Additional approved natural or artificial flavourings may be added after distillation. Colouring and sweetening is permitted.

London Gin/London Dry Gin
Made in a traditional still by redistilling a high grade of ethyl alcohol in the presence only of approved natural flavourings to a minimum strength of 70% ABV. Further ethyl alcohol may be added after distillation, provided it is of the same composition. No colouring or sweetening is permitted.

American gin
In the USA, gin can be produced "from original distillation from mash, redistillation, or mixing neutral spirits, with juniper berries and other aromatics, or with extracts from such materials. It derives its main characteristic flavour from juniper berries and is bottled at not less than 80° proof [40% ABV]".

PGI gin
Gin de Mahon (Menorca) and Vilnius Džinas (Lithuania) have protected geographical indication (PGI) status. Plymouth Gin's (*see* p.104) PGI status lapsed in 2015.

Genever
Made with ethyl alcohol/grain spirit/ distillate flavoured with juniper, which needn't be the predominant flavour. Any casks used must be no larger than 700 litres (154 gallons).

Graanjenever This is made from 100 per cent grain.

***Oude* genever** Contains a minimum of 15 per cent malt wine and no more than 20g (¾oz) sugar per litre.

Korenwijn Contains more than 51 per cent malt wine.

Oude graanjenever Contains 100 per cent grain and aged for a minimum of one year.

***Jonge* genever** Contains a maximum 15 per cent malt wine and no more than 10g (⅓oz) sugar per litre.

The following also have their own AOCs (appellation d'origine contrôlées): Hasseltse jenever, Balegemse jenever, Peket, and O'de Flander Echte Oost-Vlaamse *graaanjenever* (Belgium); *genièvre* Flandres Artois (France); Ostfriesischer Korngenever (Germany).

GIN DISTILLATION

> "Gin isn't made by molecules. It's made by people."
> Sean Harrison, master distiller, Plymouth Gin

In electronic music, the term ADSR – attack decay sustain release – is used to plot the length and properties of a note from the moment it is audible to when the sound ends. It's the same in gin distillation, with each individual constituent part cascading down into the spirit safe like a musical matrix of aromas.

When you nose a spirit run, the volatile citrus comes across first, blurring into juniper, before spices show their hand, and finally roots. In reality, because elements of one botanical are also shared by others, they overlap – as in chords rather than individual notes. To allow each botanical's full expression, distillation needs to be slow.

At the start of distillation, the "heads" containing the residue of the previous distillation are discarded. The distiller then captures the middle cut (the lightest aromas are at the start, the heaviest at the end). Before the aromas get too greasy – or at the point that suits the balance of the gin – they cut to "feints" (the unwanted "tails" at the end of a distillation). These are mixed with the "heads" and redistilled into neutral alcohol.

The distiller has to think not only of the overall balance of the gin but how each botanical interacts with its neighbour, which influences aromatic length, complexity, and evolution. Change any of the ratios between the botanicals and you alter the complex web of balances. It's a spiritous demonstration of the Buddhist principle of the interpenetration of all things. Knowing how a botanical mix behaves dictates how to distil, how slow to run the still, and when to cut.

Juniper is at the centre. Its citric notes are supported by those of citrus peels and the top notes of coriander seeds, its mid-range pine by the greenness of angelica, its tail by the warmth of spice and wood. It acts, as Desmond Payne at Beefeater says, "like the wash on a canvas".

Each of these botanicals is natural. The oil in the juniper will vary, the nature of coriander seeds change depending on where they are grown, while the intensity of the citrus peels will vary. A distiller needs to be constantly monitoring and tweaking a recipe in order to maintain consistency. This cannot be done by computer. Gin distillers are masters who know not just what each botanical smells like but how it will behave within a mixture, and then how it will perform on the palate and in a mixed drink. Gin distillers are the heroes.

The Base Spirit

Most gins are redistilled in a base spirit that has been distilled to a high strength (around 96% ABV), then mixed with water to lower the ABV to 60%. The base isn't truly neutral; it has an influence. While it's hard to pick out the difference between types of grain, all give a rounded, sometimes buttery, result. The aromatic effect of an apple, potato, or grape spirit is more apparent. The low-strength pot-still base used by some of the new gins has a greater influence, making them more of a "Hollands" style (*see* p.11). If the base changes, so does the gin.

Pot Still

The majority of gins are redistilled with their botanicals in copper pot stills. The shape of the still has an effect, with the "headspace" (the vapour-filled gap between liquid and the condenser) affecting the way in which flavour compounds rise, move, revert to liquid, and are redistilled (known as reflux). If a distiller installs a new still, she or he may have to adjust the ratios of botanicals to maintain consistency. The speed of distillation also

Gin is made by redistilling a neutral base spirit in a pot still with botanicals.

impacts on how well the oils are released, the nature of the flow, and the level of reflux. If a still is run too aggressively, there is the risk of botanicals physically coming across so, the gentler the better all round. In addition, the manner in which the botanicals are added will also influence the gin's character.

Steep and Boil

Some distillers, such as Beefeater (*see* pp.63–4) and Sipsmith (see pp.107–8), steep the botanicals for a period before distillation. This, they believe, helps fix the oils, aiding richness. Others, Gordon's (*see* pp.87–8) and Plymouth (*see* p.104), for example, only add them prior to distillation, which they attest helps to preserve brightness. The lessening of juniper's top notes in extended steeping is perhaps one reason why these gins have more citrus in their botanical mix. Others, for instance Citadelle (*see* pp.118 and 158), will macerate botanicals either individually or in combinations for different lengths of time, as each oil will release its extractives fully at a different rates.

Individual Distillation and Blending

Some distillers, such as Gin Mare (*see* p.128) and G'Vine (*see* pp.122–3), distil each botanical (or combinations) separately and then blend the distillates. This, they claim, allows them to make a more consistent product. Others insist that this loses the interaction between elements in the still. Some, for instance Tanqueray No. TEN (*see* p.111) distil one element of the final gin separately, then redistil this with the other botanicals.

Vapour Extraction

Rather than immersing the botanicals in the spirit, distillers can extract the essential oils by passing vapour through them.

Carter-Head Still

In 1831, Mary Dakin installed first a Corty head, then a Carter-Head still at her family's distillery in Warrington (*see* p.19 and p.22), now Greenall's (*see* p.89). Both had a rectifying column on top of the pot, which helped to produce a lighter, cleaner spirit. The downside was that they also stripped out most of the essential oils.

The Carter-Head and Bennett stills found at the Hendrick's distillery in Girvan, Scotland.

Berry trays – as used by Caorunn – are another method of extracting aromatics.

The solution was to place the botanicals in a copper basket that sat after the column. The vapour rushing through stripped off the oils and carried them forwards to be condensed. The technique is still in use in gins such as Bombay Sapphire (*see* pp.70–1).

The baskets are divided into segments, each packed with all the botanicals – the larger at the base, the ground ones on top. A longer "heads" run is also required, as the botanicals need to be moist before they will release their oils. The advantage of this, its proponents say, is that it gives freshness to the final gin. Its detractors say that using this method alone doesn't "fix" the aromas fully.

Berry Trays

A different technique, used for Caorunn (*see* p.78) and Boë (*see* p.68), employs a large chamber separated into trays with perforated plates onto which the botanicals are placed. The spirit vapour is then passed through.

Other Distillation Techniques

Some gins, such as The Botanist (*see* p.73), Sipsmith V.J.O.P. (*see* p.108), Hendrick's (*see* p.92), and Monkey 47 (*see* p.130) are made by combining both steeping and vapour techniques, either by having botanicals in spirit and basket or, in Hendrick's case, having one Carter-Head still and a standard pot still.

One-shot Versus Concentrate

"One-shot" distillation means that distillers collect the middle cut of a distillation, reduce it with water, and bottle it. The alternative is to add excess botanicals and then reduce the concentrated result with ethyl alcohol.

Vacuum

Although the vacuum distillation of essential oils has been around since the eighteenth century, it is a relatively new technique in gin distillation. By lowering the pressure in a still, the boiling point of all the ingredients is reduced. The oils can then be released without the botanical being "cooked", giving a fresh, clear result. Modern, glass vacuum stills, as used by Sacred (*see* p.106) and Cambridge (*see* p.77), allow the distiller to accurately capture the full range of an ingredient's aromatics. Both of these distil botanicals separately

In genever production, a thick mash is first fermented.

and then blend. An alternative, used by Oxley (*see* p.103), is to distil the botanicals together under vacuum at extremely cold temperatures.

Supercritical Fluid Extraction (SFE)
This technique has been employed by the perfume industry to isolate specific molecules but was first used in gin by Hepple, the Northumberland distillery. Increasing the pressure on CO_2 gas turns it into a "super-critical" liquid, which acts as a solvent for botanicals placed within it. By then filtering off the CO_2 and releasing the pressure, the pure essential oils - or specific compounds within them - can be accurately extracted. Some compounds that are lost in normal distillation can also be captured.

Essences
Some gins add the essence of natural botanicals post-distillation, as in the case of Hendrick's with its rose and cucumber essences (*see* p.92).

GENEVER PRODUCTION

Traditional genever production starts with making a richly flavoured and textured malt wine, customarily made from a mixed mash bill of rye, wheat and/or corn, and malted barley. Distillers such as Filliers (*see* pp.170 and 177), which produces 99 per cent of the malt wine in the Netherlands and Belgium, will run different mash bills.

The corn and/or wheat are first cooked at high temperature to soften the starches, then cooled and the rye added. After a further period of cooking, malted barley goes in. The enzymes in the barley then convert all the starches to sugar. This mash is subsequently cooled further, yeast is added, and the mixture is left to ferment for up to one week. Baker's yeast is the most commonly used, though Zuidam (*see* pp.174–6 and p.179) uses a mix of brewer's and distiller's yeast.

The resulting beer is then distilled, traditionally using pot stills (as with Zuidam), three times (similar to malt whisky production). In Zuidam's case, this gives a fruity, complex malt wine at around 70% ABV. The alternative, as used at Filliers, is to run the beer through a single column and then redistill in a pot still (similar to bourbon production). This gives a more bready, cereal-accented, and lower-strength malt wine. In both cases, the character of this base will have a significant impact in terms of mouthfeel, aroma, and flavour.

All genever distillers then redistill a portion of malt wine in pot stills, this time with botanicals – again to each distiller's/brand's recipe. Some distillers also make a separate distillate of juniper and neutral alcohol. All of these elements are then blended together. In Filliers's case, the malt wine is then either shipped to distillers or turned into genever to their customers' specifications.

This distillate can either then be reduced to bottling strength, or reduced and aged as it is. More commonly it's blended with neutral spirit, either from wheat or sugar beet molasses. The *jonge* style has a minimum of 85 per cent neutral spirit in the mix (often higher), and while *oude* must have more than 15 per cent malt wine, most contain up to 40 per cent or, in *korenwijn's* case, significantly more (*see* panel, p.39). The more malt wine, the more characterful the genever.

These *oude* blends can then be aged – most commonly for a short period, but at times for up to 20 years. Most are aged in used casks, but Zuidam uses a complex mix of new American, refill, and ex-sherry casks.

Still think gin distilling is easy? Think again!

Pot-still distillation helps to create genever's rich, bready "malt-wine" base.

HOW TO USE THIS BOOK

The challenge wasn't so much where to start but where to stop. The number of gins now available outstrips anything in the spirit's history. So, the ones chosen had to cover not only the most widely available brands but also be representative of the newer arrivals, as well as methods of production, places of origin, and styles: dry, Old Tom, cask-aged, fruit, genever; all had to be covered.

Neither was this a competition. It's pointless making a list of the "best gins" – were that to be even possible – and then not to say how they are best enjoyed. The aim here is to see how gins behave when they are consumed as they were intended to be, i.e. mixed.

There is more to drinking gin than just sloshing in tonic, however. Gin is nothing if not amenable, working with many mixers and in cocktails. How then does each respond to the challenge laid down by sweet vermouth and Campari, a double act that would make most spirits blanch? And how would they fare when more exposed in a Martini? What is the best way to enjoy fruit gins, Old Tom, cask-aged, and genever?

The key objective here is to help maximize your enjoyment so that when you are in a bar or a shop and can't find your favourite brand you will have other options. Also, as a real gin drinker, you won't just have one brand of choice but gins for different occasions and drinks. Before mixing, though, I had to get to grips with the gin itself.

SCORING SYSTEM

5* **The best.**
The perfect synthesis of gin and mixer. Everyone needs to have at least one of these.

5 **Superb.**
Elegant, effortless, and a perfect balance struck so that the gin is enhanced.

4.5 **Halfway between a superb drink and a great drink.**

4 **Great drink.**
A drink that cannot be faulted. I'd be happy to drink this all night.

3.5 **Halfway between a great drink and a good drink.**

3 **Good.**
A decently balanced drink. I'll have one. I might move on to something else afterwards.

2.5 **Halfway between a good drink and a drink that's just so-so.**

2 **So-so.**
Seek another option.

1 **Avoid.**

X **There are some gins where mixing simply doesn't work.**

The scores are given to the mix and not to the gin. Even if a gin doesn't score highly in a combination, this is not a reflection on its quality. Read the notes and find your own combinations.

TASTING GIN

Tasting gin requires a recalibration of the senses. Other spirits – rum or whisky, for example – often work on allusion, as in having an aroma that smells like, for instance, "heather", "honey", or "tropical fruit". There is no such creative latitude in gin. The aromas that you are picking up are coming from the botanicals. It's on the one hand more analytical and precise, but on the other more immersive because nosing and tasting a gin transports you to a new aromatic landscape. Let's face it, how many of us really encounter orris or angelica on a daily basis, never mind the more outré botanicals now being pressed into service? What the experience does give you, therefore, is a greater understanding and engagement with the world. These aromas aren't artificial but natural.

The way in which a gin changes on your nose mirrors exactly the progression of aromas from the still. You pick up the most volatile first, the heaviest last. You are smelling time. Relax and delve into its complexities. Rather than just being "gin", you now experience that initial burst of citrus: lemon, orange, grapefruit, or a combination. But where are the coriander seeds? How does the juniper express itself? When do the roots and spices emerge? This is a retronasal experience, meaning you detect more aromas when the gin is in your mouth. Now you can notice more clearly how one aroma blends into another, how they rise and fall.

The key is balance, not abrupt shifts from one to another. Think of how it's textured: thick, broad, light? Go back to the glass. Have the aromas changed, or simply flown off? (they should have persistence). Finally, is it juniper, citric, spicy, floral, or herbal? Having an understanding of each gin will give you an idea of how best to enjoy it.

FLAVOUR CAMPS

Each gin is an individual. At the same time, however, they also cluster themselves into societies with shared interests and characters. Grouping gins like this enables the drinker to find the brand they like and then move between gins within the same society with confidence.

Gin isn't as clear-cut as other spirits. Its complexities never allow (or shouldn't allow) one aroma to bellow its presence while its companions are reduced to mumbling in the background. Instead, there is a fascinating moiré effect. Even if juniper is forward, you cannot discount the influence of citrus or roots. Accordingly, I will sometimes give a second, qualifying term to describe a flavour camp.

Juniper

These gins are the most "traditional", even if some come from new makers, allowing the juniper its fullest expression. The initial aroma will therefore be filled with pine, heather, and lavender, which will continue to have a major say through the palate. If you want to understand where gin came from, or even what juniper smells like, then start here.

Citric

Citrus peels began to be widely used in the mid- to late nineteenth century, and the classic examples of this camp come from around that time, but again this isn't a character that's restricted to a single time period. Here, the aroma is given lift by citrus peels, but coriander seeds also move further forward, though juniper retains importance. These aren't so much light as fresh.

Spicy

A more modern style, where coriander seed's pepperiness is apparent, as are its cohorts cassia/cinnamon and peppers. The juniper has been dialled back.

Floral

A significant New Gin camp, these gins have a fragrant, perfumed aspect, sometimes coming from flowers in the botanical mix, or by dint of the juniper and roots being scaled back – sometimes to little more than a trace. Gins with a herbal element, though slightly bolder, fall into this camp.

Uncategorized

As Old Tom, cask-aged, and flavoured gins and genever have their own individual styles, they haven't been subdivided into flavour camps.

The king of mixed drinks, a Negroni must always be well balanced.

NEGRONI RATIOS

Some say cocktail ratios are writ in stone and that altering them is the equivalent of doodling rude pictures in the margins of a Bible. Why try to change something that is as near as dammit perfect? Because it's human nature and also, in this case, because of the need to demonstrate the two prime directives of any mixed drink: complexity and balance.

The Negroni is a gin drink. It's also a gin drink with some pretty noisy companions who can come blundering into the bar singing at the tops of their voices, the vermouth slurring in a baritone, the Campari behaving like a flame-haired drag queen. It might be entertaining, but they just need to keep the noise down a bit. Hitting the ideal balance is tricky not only because of their presence but because every gin is different. Some are bold, others are discreet. While Tanqueray can hold its own at a classic ratio (*see* p.110), a delicate gin like Bombay Sapphire is lost (*see* p.70–1). Therefore, the ratio needs to be adjusted to make a balanced gin drink. All ratios refer to gin:vermouth:Campari.

N1

1:1:1 This classic ratio is perfect for bigger and juniper-forward gins either because the gin is either big enough to hold its own, or forces its companions into line.

N2

1½:1:1 This ratio suits citric gins (and some others). The key here is that freshness and top notes have been retained and boosted.

N3

2:1:½ A ratio that's deal for spicier/herbal gins whose mid-palate bite is the key to character. Here, the Campari's volume needs to be turned down otherwise its own spice and bitterness causes a clash.

N4

2:1:1 A mix for the light, floral group, with the gin element upped. While it may seem counterintuitive to increase the Campari, here its top notes add to the balance.

MIXERS

Tonic Water

Quinine, Fiammetta Rocco points out in her book *The Miraculous Fever-Tree*, was "the modern world's first real pharmaceutical drug". Originally extracted from Peruvian cinchona bark in the 1630s, it was initially taken in powdered form in wine and used to treat fevers. A century later it was being administered as a tincture and was hailed as a cure-all. In 1809, during the Napoleonic Wars, a British expedition to Walcheren in the Netherlands was struck down with malaria, demonstrating the need for the Army to carry supplies of quinine. In 1823, the Philadelphia-based firm Rosengarten & Sons started producing quinine extract on a commercial scale, which was then given in pill form to workers in malarial zones. The British Army, however, stuck with the liquid form and, by the 1850s, in India, troops were countering quinine's extreme bitterness with sugar – and gin. As a response, in 1858, Erasmus Bond made the first commercial tonic water, followed 20 years later by Jacob Schweppe.

As the mix became popular, so the tonic water had its quinine content reduced to a level where it only provided flavour. Why did the G&T remain a British drink until the 1960s? Maybe it was because the Americans took their quinine in pill form.

Fever-Tree, for me, is the tonic that enhances gin perfectly. The quinine comes from the Rwanda/Congo border, and the bitter orange from Tanzania. Sweetened with natural sugar (rather than aspartame or saccharine), the carbonation is smooth rather than coarse. It's a clean, lightly citric, balanced mixer.

Fever-Tree's tonic has the ideal balance between bubbles, sweetness, and quinine.

Sicilian Lemonade

A perverse choice? Hear me out. I started out with gin and Schweppes Bitter Lemon. Then, when in Spain, I discovered the joys of gin and Fanta Limón. Next came an appreciation of the simple early gin drinks that used fresh lemon juice. When I triangulated the positives of each, in the centre sat Fever-Tree's Sicilian Lemonade. It's more tart than Fanta, more lemony than bitter lemon, less sharp than juice. Game over.

Vermouth

I see vermouth and gin as evidence of Einstein's theory of "spooky action at a distance". Though separated, they have always been linked; when one moves, so does the other. If gin's history (and name) is that of juniper's, then vermouth's saga follows wormwood's (*Wermut* in German) use as a curative herb. Its spiritual home is Piedmont – specifically Turin – where wormwood-infused wine ("hippocras") became a speciality from the sixteenth century, though discoveries of residues within bronze vessels in China show that wine has been aromatized with herbs and spices for at least 3,000 years. "Modern" vermouth dates from 1786 in Turin when Antonio Carpano launched his first version. In time it spread beyond Piedmont, over the Alps to Chambéry and the southern Rhône where, in 1813, Joseph Noilly started making his French version. By the mid-nineteenth century, vermouths were being exported, though in the USA it remained a specialist taste until mixologists began mixing with it. When paired with gin, the latter changed forever. Without each other, both would have remained interesting specialities; together, they took over the world.

Vermouth is made by adding botanicals (which must include wormwood) to a wine base that itself has been fortified. Each producer has its own secret botanical recipe, but the following are commonly used: angelica, aniseed, calamus, cardamom, clove, elder, genepy, gentian, lemon balm, liquorice, orris root, rhubarb, rosemary, vanilla, and tonka beans. No wonder why it works so well with gin. Vermouth not only bonds with gin but contributes sweetness; it softens the spirit's attack yet adds gin's punch to its delivery.
The combination is greater than the sum of the parts.

After extensive (and satisfying) testing, the following sweet and dry vermouths were used for the cocktails.

Sweet

Cocchi Storico came out top of the sweet vermouths tested, tied with **La Quintinye Rouge**, and with **Martini**

Fever-Tree's Sicilian lemonade is a versatile mixer.

Noilly Prat is the ideal vermouth for Dry Martinis.

Rosso running a close third. The Cocchi firm was founded in 1891 by Giulio Cocchi in Asti, Italy, and their Storico Vermouth di Torino is a re-creation of the firm's original recipe, based on Moscato. It has a highly complex nose with cacao, mint, Seville orange, nutmeg, ginger, and clove, and a classic bittersweet delivery with wormwood, gentian, and rhubarb. It's long and layered.

La Quintinye Rouge from the Charente is based on a blend of local white wine and (red) Pineau de Charentes with 28 botanicals. It has vanilla, cherry, prune, liquorice, orange peel, and clove on the nose, while the palate starts fruitily sweet before cinchona and wormwood come through. It's pure and balanced.

Dry (aka "French")

Noilly Prat Original Dry was a clear winner, but the more vinous **Vya Extra Dry** and **La Quintinye Extra Dry** also performed well. Noilly is based on a blend of Picpoul and Clairette wines that are first aged in tuns, then spend a year weathering and oxidizing outdoors prior to being fortified and having 20 botanicals slowly added. It has a chamomile/elderflower-like floral note, with herbs, minerality, almond, and a balanced acid/bitter palate.

Campari is the noisiest member of the Negroni gang.

Campari

This legendary aperitif bitters was created in the 1860s in Novara in the Piedmont region of Italy by Gaspare Campari who, in another "spooky action" with gin, originally called it *Bitter all'Uso d'Holanda* ("bitters in the Dutch style"). Campari's recipe is a secret and is made by macerating its botanicals in water and alcohol, then sweetened and coloured – originally with cochineal. It was first mixed with amaro vermouth to make the Torino-Milano aperitif, then with Martini Rosso to make the Milano-Torino, before being lengthened with soda to make the Americano. Then, in 1920, Count Camillo Negroni entered the Bar Casoni (*see* p.186) and things changed forever.

It's dense and bitter – maybe gentian, calamus, and angelica with bergamot-like notes. Concentrated on the tongue, its bitterness is softened by a satisfying citric sweetness.

Remember the G&T? A GIN drink!

BASIC RECIPES

G&T

This mix is, probably, the most popular long mixed drink in the world. The dry bite of quinine, the lightly citric sweetness, the susurration of bubbles anticipating your sigh as you take the first sip, carrying the gin's fragrance towards your nose – go on, you need one now. Admit it.

Today, the G&T is enjoying a renaissance, the trigger for which came thanks to the explosion of interest in gin among a new generation of Spanish drinkers. It was in Spain where I first came across the concept of drinking G&T after a meal, which there means around midnight. It revives the taste buds, clears the head of Rioja, and sets you up for the next stage of the evening's entertainment. The serve was also different. None of the dribble of gin, flaccid lemon, watery ice, and oceans of tonic as served in the British pub; Spanish bartenders were joyously heavy handed, delivering a massive shot of gin, an afterthought of tonic, and good hard ice. In recent times, the Spanish serve has now extended to presenting it in a large balloon wine glass.

I have taken that Spanish approach here, but calmed it just a little. In all of the examples, the ratio I used was 2:1 tonic:gin. If that remained too strong, the ratio was lengthened to 3:1. The same principle was applied to the Sicilian Lemonade.

Remember, mixers are there to lengthen and enhance and not to obliterate. Use small bottles where possible; large bottles are only to be used if they are emptied in one session. If you see a bartender reaching for a mixing gun, stop them and order a different drink.

Martini

There is plenty about the Martini later on, but I approached these with the belief that this is a gin and vermouth drink and the latter has a role to play. In their *Guide to Vermouth & Other Apéritifs*, cocktail historians Anistatia Miller and Jared Brown persuasively argue that Martinis only became drier because people forgot to treat vermouth as a wine and let it sit and go sour on the shelf. Gin and fresh vermouth is, however, a fantastic combination. Accordingly, these all started out as 4:1 gin:vermouth. If the latter was dominating, then I would lengthen the mix to 5:1. Occasionally, some were best "naked", with no vermouth at all.

Negroni

The rationale behind the different ratios of Negronis has already been laid out (*see* p.49). But what I haven't yet mentioned – and this applies to the Martini as well – is how important temperature is to these drinks. Vermouth should be kept in the fridge, and it should be used quickly (buy half bottles), as should the Campari. Ideally, the gin comes straight out of the freezer. The difference will astound you... and impress your friends.

Other Mixes

A different tack I tried was with genever and Old Tom, cask-rested, and fruit gins. I know Old Tom is versatile, but I was intrigued to see how it behaved in a nineteenth-century way. The same went for cask-rested gin and genever (which doesn't get on with dry vermouth anyway). So in came the Gin Cocktail, Gin Fizz, and the Martinez. When the last was too vermouth-dominated, I switched to the Turf Club.

GIN COCKTAIL

There are a large number of recipes for this drink, but I used the oldest and simplest.

30ml (1fl oz) gin

5ml (⅙fl oz) simple syrup or gomme (*see* p.188)

dash of Angostura, Boker's, or orange bitters, depending on preference

Stir all the ingredients over ice and strain into a chilled coupette glass.

The Gin Fizz (or Collins) is a hugely refreshing mix.

GIN FIZZ

This same recipe was used for the fruit Gin Fizzes.

30ml (1fl oz) gin

1½ tsp fresh lemon juice

1 tsp simple syrup or gomme (*see* p.188)

soda water, to top up

Shake all the ingredients, bar the soda water, with ice and strain into a chilled cocktail glass. Top up with soda water.

MARTINEZ

30ml (1fl oz) sweet vermouth

15ml (½fl oz) gin

½ tsp Maraschino

dash of Angostura, Boker's, or orange bitters, depending on preference

Stir all the ingredients over ice and strain into a chilled cocktail glass.

TURF CLUB

45ml (1½fl oz) gin

45ml (1 1½fl oz) sweet vermouth

2 dashes of Angostura, Boker's, or orange bitters, depending on preference

Stir all the ingredients over ice and strain into a chilled cocktail glass.

GINS

"The funny thing about my gin," one distiller said to me, "is that I am the only person to know what it really tastes like." This seemed a strange comment to make, as the brand he was talking about is hardly unknown around the world. What he meant was that no matter how much people loved his gin, the first thing they would do is take it and make a mixed drink with it. Gin isn't a spirit that people sit and sip neat – the only people I know who take it neat or with a drop of water are, er, gin distillers. He was, of course, right.

Understanding the personality of a gin gives you an idea of how best to enjoy it. There are some gins that seem made to be drunk long. There are others that only blossom as a Negroni or a Martini. There are lunchtime gins and early evening gins. There are *digestif* gins and, dare I say it, there are breakfast gins. There are 120 of them waiting for you here, all tried in a number of ways. It's time to dive in.

BRITISH

The gins that follow here are all made in Britain (not just England, but also in Scotland and Wales) and typify the style that most of us are most familiar with. Here are the big brands, here are some old stagers, but here also are newer arrivals, the advance troops of gin's new wave.

It's easy to be caught up in the excitement of a new gin appearing every week – give it five years and every town in Britain will have its own gin – but what the tasting showed is that it would be wrong to dismiss the old nineteenth-century brands in preference to the bright, shiny, and new. Big brands are popular in the long term not because of marketing but because of their inherent quality. At some point in a marketing-led brand's life there will be a drinker pointing out that the emperor has no clothes. A high-quality gin has no such fears.

Here's another thing. Don't be seduced by the number of botanicals listed on a bottle. Taste the gin. Is it complex? Is it balanced? Do these botanicals give extra character and depth, or are they window dressing?

You will certainly find some new favourites here – I did – but you will also hopefully rediscover the qualities of some established brands.

BOTANICALS

Undeclared but include: Juniper • Orange peel • Elderflower

6 O'CLOCK GIN 43% ABV

Made by liqueur specialists Bramley and Gage (*see* p.167), the inspiration for this gin came from director Michael Kain's great-grandfather who, every evening, would sit down at 6 o'clock with a G&T to contemplate the day's events and plan for the future. Given that he became a successful engineer, the routine clearly worked. According to Kain, his ancestor's watchword was "balance, poise, and precision", which sums up what any fine gin should be about.

The nose opens with a slightly baked earth note and a floral aroma, backed up with discreet juniper, sweet orange, and a little marzipan. Well balanced and precise, it has sufficient roots and spices to stop things flying away. Water brings out coriander and some almost biscuity complexity. The palate is sweet, intense, and quite weighty, with clean citric elements on top of a lightly drying mid-palate. That floral-citric note carries through to the finish.

FLAVOUR CAMP Citric	
3	**G&T:** Big aromatic lift to start, but the quinine is quick to show its hand. Carbonation adds drive, but it feels a little short.
3.5	**With Sicilian Lemonade:** A cashew-like nuttiness develops. A little hot on the palate, but has some density and length.
3.5	**Negroni:** N2 More spices and bittering roots come into play with an eruption of fruits in the middle of the tongue before some geranium makes itself known. A little conflicted.
4	**Martini:** Six o'clock is Martini time for me, so how does it perform? I'd take it out to 5:1 to stop the vermouth adding more heft and allow the aromatics to develop. Remains intense and dry.

BOTANICALS

Juniper • Orris root • Coriander seeds • Sweet orange peel • Lemon peel • Hibiscus flower

ADNAMS COPPER HOUSE

40% ABV

Distilled by John McCarthy at Southwold (on the Suffolk coast, East Anglia) brewer Adnams's brand new (well, 2010) still house, this was the firm's first foray into spirits (they have since moved on to whisky, vodka, absinthe, apple spirit, triple sec, and fernet) and is a modernist take on the traditional. Heavy florals predominate thanks to the hibiscus, with just a hint of elderflower, sultana, and a herbal edge. With water it gets fatter and juicier, allowing sage-like juniper and coriander to show. The palate tastes like it noses, reminding me of North African cooking for some reason – flowers, sweet spices, dried fruits, citrus, fresh herb. The finish is long and heavy.

FLAVOUR CAMP Floral/Spicy

3.5	**G&T:** As a slightly cooked quality comes out at 1:2, this is best lengthened to add balance; the juniper then begins to come through.
4	**With Sicilian Lemonade:** The aromatics – especially that heavy floral note – are more ideally matched with a fresher mixer. Again, some lengthening is beneficial.
4	**Negroni:** N4 The florals are preserved by allowing the Campari and vermouth to stay in more restrained mode – to the drink's benefit. Clean with a new cherry note, and a refreshingly bittersweet finish.
3.5	**Martini:** Its heavy perfume is retained, but the chill and the vermouth help to calm down its more exuberant qualities. Becomes drier and therefore better balanced. I'd have it short, quick, and hard.

BOTANICALS

Juniper • Coriander seeds • Orris root • Angelica root • Cassia bark • Liquorice root • Hops • Lavender • Elderflower • Rose hips • Samphire • Lemon peel • Bitter orange peel • Kaffir lime leaves

ANNO 43% ABV

When colleagues Dr. Andrew Reason and Dr. Norman Lewis took early retirement from GlaxoSmithKline in 2011, they knew they weren't ready to spend the rest of their lives playing golf. As research scientists they understood distillation, loved spirits, and figured that making gin would be a fun thing to do. Within a few months they had a Christian Carl still installed in their premises in Marden, Kent, and were planning a botanical recipe that reflected their home county, hence the addition of hops, lavender, elderflower, rose hips, and samphire to the mix.

The nose is light, with a clean, fruity top note that drifts towards heavy florals and a slightly mineral edge. The citrus comes through with a touch of lavender and light juniper. It's balanced, with some charm. Water brings out lightly waxed fruits and gooseberry. The palate is fresh with lavender, with dry roots balancing a velvety feel.

FLAVOUR CAMP Fragrant/fruity	
3	**G&T:** Fruit and flower forward with the tonic for some reason. Clean and crisp, but a little short.
3.5	**With Sicilian Lemonade:** A jab of extra citrus on top of this fragrant mélange. Good juiciness and a clean palate. A long summer drink.
3.5	**Negroni:** N3 Clean with some of the hoppiness now coming through alongside bitter peels. Shows good balance with a little touch of jelly babies. Easy-going and fun.
4	**Martini:** Pure fruits, wild herbs, and more of that mineral element, which adds interest. Soft with excellent penetration and length. Well worth a look.

BOTANICALS

Juniper • Coriander seeds • Orange peel • Cinnamon • Clove • Cardamom

BATHTUB GIN 43.3% ABV

I must express bewilderment as to why you would want to name a premium product after a style of gin that was famous for its toxicity. There is nothing about the bathtub here. Rather, this is some justification for the ancient art of cold compounding. The botanicals are simply steeped in high-proof grain spirit, which is why it has a slightly daffodil-like hue. Whether the mysterious producer Professor Cornelius Ampleforth (*see also* p.154) does all of this in his bath is not known.

The nose is crisp and bone dry with forward juniper, and coriander in its more lemony personality coming behind, alongside oil of clove, cinnamon, and mulled spices – which is why it works well in Warm Gin Punch (*see* p.191) – plus a nuttiness (maybe from the spirit) at the end. The palate starts calmly before drying in the mid-palate. The mulling spices then kick through a little chaotically. It's a little aggressive, so needs water.

FLAVOUR CAMP Spicy	
3	**G&T:** Clean with a dry spicy kick and decent persistence. A decent G&T.
3.5	**With Sicilian Lemonade:** Works a little better, as it has a better length thanks to the citrus, which manages to control those mental spices. A decent balance is achieved.
3.5	**Negroni:** N3 Immensely aromatic, with the power of a prop forward heading towards the try line. The palate is a little flat, but the twist of orange helps.
4	**Martini:** Good. Those dry spices leap out from the start, but also match well with the subtle accents of the vermouth. A 5:1 ratio gives a more classical frame with lots of retronasal action, but for me it loses balance.

BOTANICALS

Juniper • Coriander seeds • Liquorice root • Orris root • Seville orange • Lemon peel • Bitter almond • Angelica root

BEEFEATER 47% ABV (export strength)

James Burrough was originally a pharmacist who, in 1863, bought John Taylor's gin distillery in Cale Street, Chelsea, in central London. His Beefeater brand was launched in 1876. Since 1958, when the firm's Lambeth distillery closed, it has been distilled in Kennington, close enough to The Oval cricket ground for its rooftop to be rattled by a well-hit six.

This is a discreetly complex gin. Juniper is there in piney guise, while coriander melds its citric notes to the peels – and it's this freshness that predominates. The angelica flowers add a light hoppy note, and the dryness is balanced by the acidity. Juniper is a constant presence. This is the perfect lunchtime or early evening gin, carrying with it memories of an endless summer. Go for this export-strength version (47% ABV), if you can find it, in preference to the standard 40% ABV offering.

FLAVOUR CAMP Citric/Juniper

5	**G&T:** The gin's freshness has been retained, along with its bracing acidity, giving you a whistle-clean rendition. The tonic never strays into bitter territory. One to make you exhale happily.
5*	**With Sicilian Lemonade:** As you might expect, there is a massive citric impact here that's a bit like sticking your head into a lemon tree at harvest time. It works, with length and a joyful persistence.
5	**Negroni:** N2 This ratio helps preserve that intensity, while the juniper locks in behind with the vermouth. Herbal and pure, with juicy weight. Exemplary stuff.
5*	**Martini:** Pleasingly oily with excellent balance. The juniper becomes bolder initially, but there is enough citric activity to balance. Crisp and ultra clean. Lunchtime/early evening.

BOTANICALS

Juniper • Coriander seeds • Angelica seeds and root • Seville orange • Lemon peel • Liquorice root • Bitter almond • Orris root • Grapefruit • Sencha tea • Chinese green tea

BEEFEATER 24 45% ABV

This is when G&T becomes gin and tea. Beefeater's master distiller Desmond Payne starts with the classic Beefeater base (though in different ratios) and then adds in grapefruit peel, Japanese Sencha tea, and Chinese green tea. The cut-off point here is very high, as the tea starts to stew quite quickly. Beefeater is fresh, complex, and citric anyway, and here the precise sweet hit of grapefruit adds further lift before the Seville peels are detectable.

Juniper brings pine, while the grassiness is coming from the Sencha. Water makes it subtly piney with some green celery notes and gentle roots. The palate is ripe, subtle, and long with the teas coming through in the centre of the tongue. It's a very confident new gin.

FLAVOUR CAMP Citric	
4	**G&T:** Fragrant, summery, and cool. A very fresh afternoon libation, thank you very much.
4	**With Sicilian Lemonade:** More citrus anyone? It works - it could easily overload - but the lemon/grapefruit interface achieves an excellent balance.
4.5	**Negroni:** N2 It's here where you begin to notice the teas, adding fresh green/grassy notes and giving the mix a fragrant lift to the mid-palate. The volume of the Campari maybe needs to be tweaked down a little, but it's a minor detail.
5	**Martini:** Again, the teas emerge - that fresh green chlorophyll note linking with the herbal notes of the vermouth. It needs to be 5:1, otherwise this accord doesn't work.

BOTANICALS

Juniper • Coriander seeds • Angelica root • Cubeb berries • Basil • Sage • Lavender • Kaffir lime leaves

BERKELEY SQUARE 40% ABV

After the success of Bloom (*see* p.67), Joanne Moore of Greenall's (*see also* pp.89, 94, and 102) went back to the garden to pick some fresh herbs – basil, lavender, and sage – and then threw in Kaffir lime leaves. The delicate herbs are placed in a muslin bag and given 24 hours' steeping to extract their aromas. Distillation is very gentle to stop any stewing. The nose is highly aromatized with some lavender (also coming from juniper), followed by a huge basil hit. It then becomes limey. All very up and crisp, this is a herbal infusion that takes gin into a new and different dimension. The palate is super clean and extremely soft, with the herbal elements becoming slightly shy, and it's well balanced with water. Not too dry, too sweet, or too herbal, this is a great new gin.

FLAVOUR CAMP Floral/Herbal

3	**G&T:** I'm not convinced that the tonic adds anything because the flavours are so upfront. It's a decent drink, but there is no enhancement here.
4	**With Sicilian Lemonade:** The herbs are calmed down and an excellent balance is struck between the mixer and the complexities of the gin. Have it long, or as a Collins (*see* p.188) where the impact is more subtle.
4	**Negroni:** N4 Good citrus and herbs, moving into a minty area. Those herbs have a natural accord with the other ingredients and the drink's sweetness bolsters up the mid-palate.
5	**Martini:** A wine aromatized with herbs proves a natural partner, with little puffs of herbs being released at regular intervals. There is even a little lavendery juniper hit at the end. Like it!

BOTANICALS

Juniper • Coriander seeds • Citrus peel • Liquorice root • Cinnamon • Nutmeg • Angelica root • Sea thrift • Marsh marigold • Meadowsweet

BLACKWOODS VINTAGE DRY GIN 2012 40% ABV

The saga of Blackwoods is suitably Norse in nature. Although its original owners claimed otherwise, it was never made on Shetland, even if Shetland botanicals are used. To confuse matters, there is now a distillery on Unst that is making gin, but it's not this one. The controversy over its origins should not detract from the simple fact that it's good juice. It's herbal and clean on the nose, with citrus upfront and a honeyed, nigh-on buttery edge of meadowsweet, then very gentle, almost floral juniper notes. It becomes more overtly citric and maintains fresh vibrancy on the palate before some pepperiness comes in, quickly followed by cassia and coriander before the flowers and citrus return.

FLAVOUR CAMP Citric

3.5	**G&T:** Good and attractive, with the mixer giving some vitality and a deepening of the base notes. A decent mix.
4	**With Sicilian Lemonade:** As you would expect, there is a natural link here, with a fresh acidic energy and a decent length. Appetizing.
3	**Negroni:** N2 The dusty botanicals begin to show here. It's quite tight with the bitter peels coming through, but seems slightly undecided whether it wants to mellow down or remain sassy.
3.5	**Martini:** Good at 4:1 because this is a gin that benefits from the little nudges that the vermouth provides. The herbal elements link with those in the gin, and while the spirit remains muted, there is a cleanliness and bite to it.

BOTANICALS

Juniper • Coriander seeds • Angelica root • Cubeb berries • Honeysuckle • Chamomile • Pomelo peel

BLOOM 40% ABV

This was Greenall's master distiller Joanne Moore's first venture into working with distillates of flowers (*see also* p.65). Here, chamomile and honeysuckle are given a further delicate lift by the addition of pomelo rather than the traditional citrus fruits. The aroma is very light and discreet with a honeyed touch before zingy citrus comes through, followed by a cool menthol note. Everything is quite subtle, adding a meadow-like calmness to the proceedings. On the palate there are tisane notes and chamomile tea, alongside the almost evanescent perfume. Water shows that there is juniper and violet growing in this garden, and allows the spirit to spread and anchor itself. It's really well handled, with no stewing of the flowers.

FLAVOUR CAMP Floral

4.5	**G&T:** Becomes very floral and springs into life. The perfect, cool summery G&T, like sticking your head in a bride's bouquet, if that weren't rude. Which it is.
2.5	**With Sicilian Lemonade:** There is less sympathy here, as the lemonade gives too much citrus and kills the pomelo. Overwhelmed.
3.5	**Negroni:** N4 This is a big ask for such a delicate gin with the Campari always dominating. A more radical solution to the classic Negroni ingredients might be better. Try Aperol and rose vermouth?
4.5	**Martini:** You need this gin to show itself fully, so the vermouth should be scaled right back. 5:1 is ideal for me here because its influence is subtle, but also linked directly to the garden blossom. A lovely drink.

BOTANICALS

Juniper • Coriander seeds • Cardamom • Angelica root • Ginger • Almond • Orris root • Cassia bark • Liquorice root • Orange peel • Lemon peel • Cubeb berries

BOË 47% ABV

This is made by Ian MacMillan at the Deanston Distillery near Stirling, Scotland, who started his career working in London at the Booth's gin plant. The apparent wispiness of many of the new Scottish gins makes me want to draw a parallel between them and Glasgow indie bands – they're charming but can come across as being a little, well, lightweight. This is citrus-led and aromatic, with some delicate fennel and the juniper in the background. In time there is peppermint, lemon peel, ginger, and cinnamon. The palate is winter fresh with an intense mint note mixed in with floral notes and juniper berries. Like those bands, you need to look beyond your initial impression.

FLAVOUR CAMP Floral/Fragrant

3.5	**G&T:** With the tonic, there is a slightly fruit note that develops alongside the lemon. It's clean but needs more energy. There is, however, persistence of aroma.
3.5	**With Sicilian Lemonade:** Initially the mixer takes over, but then the gin kicks in with its citrus lead. Decent and best as a Fizz, where there is more bunched-up aggression.
3	**Negroni:** N4 Remains light and now has more of a herbal twist to it. There is a good enough balance here with decent juniper coming across. It's fine.
3.5	**Martini:** The vermouth needs to be controlled here, so I'd take it out to 5:1, which seems to accentuate the sweetness rather than the overtly botanical elements. This spicier drive gives it good balance.

BOTANICALS

Juniper • Lemon peel • Coriander seeds • Orris root • Angelica root • Bitter almond • Liquorice root • Cassia bark

BOMBAY DRY 40% ABV

The downside of Bombay Sapphire's success is how its considerably older brother has been sidelined, which is a pity in my view, as this is an excellent traditional gin. Its recipe is based on the one created by Thomas Dakin in Warrington in 1761 (*see* p.89) and then refined further in terms of production in the 1830s when the distillery installed the then new Carter-Head still (*see* pp.42–3). It was named Bombay in 1960 when New York lawyer Alain Subin decided to break into the drinks world.

A sound, if slightly lighter, LDG approach is shown here with juniper and dusty woods upfront, alongside orange peel, marzipan, and a sweet spiciness. Water shows a baked earth note typical of orris and pine. On the palate it is surprisingly sweet to start, before white pepper sneezes in, followed quickly by citrus to balance things out. The texture is silky, with the heavier elements massing on the end.

FLAVOUR CAMP Juniper

3.5	**G&T:** Rich and well balanced, with a pleasant peppery catch in the middle adding interest. Decent persistence.
5	**With Sicilian Lemonade:** Lovely lift that adds another element to the mix, which is always good news. Very well balanced in the centre. Excellent.
4	**Negroni:** N1 This ratio allows the spicy, almost gingery pepperiness to come through more strongly while the juniper and orris hold their own. Medium weight and with character. A good drink.
3.5	**Martini:** Unctuous, rich, and thick with massive flavour delivery. It may lack some finesse, but it has a certain boisterous charm.

BOTANICALS

Juniper • Coriander seeds • Angelica root • Liquorice root • Orris root • Cassia bark • Almond • Lemon peel • Cubeb berries • Grains of paradise

BOMBAY SAPPHIRE 40% ABV

Where would gin be without Sapphire? Conceivably, still in the doldrums. After all, this is the brand that kick-started the gin renaissance by daring to make the drink in a new lighter guise (*see* p.69). Traditionalists may dismiss Sapphire, but that's unfair. It does what it sets out to do and does it well. While it is delicate on the nose, it has an understated intensity when you look carefully. Citrus, pepper, and warm sweet spices are most prominent together with leafy angelica and a background note of juniper, alongside a cooked vegetal element. Lacy in texture, the peels become more prominent on the tongue, bursting forward like schoolchildren released into the playground. Think of lemon cheesecake and you're not far off. In time, the pepper becomes more prominent.

FLAVOUR CAMP Floral/Fragrant

2.5	**G&T:** Clean and very spicy, green, and immediate. By the time you take your second sip the aromatic burst has gone, so keep it short and quick.
3.5	**With Sicilian Lemonade:** The mixer gently steers the gin, lengthening its aromatic persistence. Quite punchy on the tongue. Best as a sharpener, or a Fizz.
4	**Negroni:** N4 This ratio allows the gin to express itself when in the presence of two heavyweights. Pleasingly fragrant, exotically spiced, and lightly peppery with a little bitterness to offset the sweet mid-palate.
4	**Martini:** Sapphire's delicacy necessitates a drier ratio. So 5:1, even 6:1 is better, when you can appreciate the gin's complexity and where the slower release of aromatics, thanks to the low temperature, finally gives it some length.

BOTANICALS

Juniper • Coriander seeds • Angelica root • Liquorice root • Orris root • Cassia bark • Almond • Lemon peel • Cubeb berries • Grains of paradise • Lemon grass • Vietnamese black peppercorns

BOMBAY SAPPHIRE EAST

42% ABV

Here we have the classic Sapphire mix, but with further additions of lemon grass and Vietnamese black peppercorns to take it into Southeast Asia. The black pepper is certainly there on the nose, while the lemon grass is slightly more shy, preferring to hang around the back of the bike sheds with the citrus and juniper. There are some cooked vegetal notes and then menthol, pepper, and low juniper. The palate is clean and restrained.

FLAVOUR CAMP Spicy

2.5	**G&T:** Fresh and peppery, but it fades pretty quickly.
3.5	**With Sicilian Lemonade:** A better mix. OK, it's light but in the Sapphire mould, and while I would have expected lemon and lemon grass to be a blast, it's slightly more laid-back. Just needs a little extra zest to drive things forward.
3.5	**Negroni:** N3 The fragrant pepperiness comes through very cleanly. A tad astringent, but the lemon grass now begins to have a bit of a play along with the delicate spices. Decent.
3.5	**Martini:** A better delivery especially when made drier, i.e. 5:1. Clean, with decent intensity. It dries and then seems to fizz with spices at the end, which is what you want. Altogether the most successful.

BOTANICALS

Not fully declared but include: Juniper • nutmeg • sage • rosemary

BOODLES 40% ABV (45.2% export strength)

This old brand started life in the nineteenth century as the house gin at Boodle's gentleman's club in St James's, London. These days it is made at Beefeater (*see* pp.63–4) and destined pretty much exclusively for the USA. It is unusual in having no citrus botanicals in the mix. The nose is surprisingly gentle and as quiet as the Members' Room after lunch. It's all very well mannered, with a citric jag (possibly from coriander), some lavender, violet, rosemary, black tea, and sage-like juniper acting as an underpinning. With water it becomes juicy in its attack with a general softness taking charge. On the palate it's pretty sweet to kick off with, but that's immediately countered by a surprising astringency. It's crisp, firmer, and more rooty than you would initially judge. The gentlemen of the club aren't that soft-hearted after all.

FLAVOUR CAMP Fruity/Juniper

3	**G&T:** Very spicy on the nose – there doesn't seem to be a need for any adulteration here. The tonic adds some structure and its sweetness fights against the bitterness. Angelica and liquorice come through.
3.5	**With Sicilian Lemonade:** The addition of citrus suggests that this should be a no-brainer, and while it delivers beautifully in that regard, the palate lacks the lift to give the mix momentum.
3.5	**Negroni:** N2 As the nose suggests, this is very polite and well bred. Wholly pleasant and seamless with a certain minty, menthol edge, but it lacks a spark.
3.5	**Martini:** This needs to be at 5:1, as the vermouth has to play a near-invisible background role, just enough to add energy. But it remains calm and vey reliable, if not hugely exciting.

BOTANICALS

22 locally foraged botanicals: Juniper • Apple mint • Spearmint • Water mint • Downy birch • Chamomile • Creeping thistle • Elder • Gorse flower • Heather flower • Hawthorn flower • Lady's bedstraw • Lemon balm • Meadowsweet • Mugwort • Red clover • White clover • Sweet cicely • Bog myrtle • Tansy • Thyme • Wood sage • Cassia bark • Peppermint • Angelica root • Coriander seeds • Cinnamon bark • Lemon peel • Orange peel • Liquorice root • Orris root

THE BOTANIST 46% ABV

The idea of a whisky distillery making gin may seem unusual, but it's more commonplace than you might think. Springbank (*see* pp.76 and 101) does it, as does Balmenach (*see* p.78) and Deanston (*see* p.68), while the Girvan (*see* p.92) and Cameronbridge (*see* p.87) grain plants also have gin distilleries. Making gin in the home of smoky whisky is slightly more of a surprise, but Bruichladdich sells itself as a "progressive Hebridean Distiller" and what could be more progressive than making a gin using native Islay botanicals? Gentle, rich, and oily on the nose, it becomes like a walk in the woods – soft fruits, heavy blossom, pine trees, sage, dry barks, and a honeyed element, then chamomile, some bilberry, raspberry leaf, wild herbs, and ground spices. Complex in other words. The palate is soft with powdery mixed spices and a slight chocolaty finish. I would love to see an aged variant.

FLAVOUR CAMP Juniper/Fruity	
4.5	**G&T:** Initially slightly closed by the tonic, but perks up in the mouth, with good length, solid juniper, and some fragrance.
3	**With Sicilian Lemonade:** Broad and showing good balance, but maybe just a bit too dry. A little harsh on the mid-palate.
4	**Negroni:** N3 The vermouth has been dialled back, allowing more of a scented nose to emerge. This has depth, richness, and good integration.
5	**Martini:** Really oily, with gentle vermouth allied to the more herbaceous elements. I prefer it at 5:1 where the complexity of the gin shows.

BOTANICALS

Undeclared but 8 used

BRECON BOTANICALS 43% ABV

Currently the only Welsh gin, this hails from the Penderyn whisky distillery in the foothills of the Brecon Beacons. The nose is very subtle, delicate, and perfumed with low juniper, putting it firmly in the New Gin camp. In time, there is a light aniseed note mixed with pine, sage, heather, and bergamot. It's all very clean, crisp, and discreet before the palate brings out a slight floral/herbal/honeyed note alongside some berry-like fruit. A clever complex gin, it seems to present a new aroma with every sniff. The palate is gentle, clean, and soft, with most of the action coming in the middle of the tongue where the peels kick in and the juniper slowly distributes its flavours. It dries to almost gentian-like levels on the finish, adding crispness.

FLAVOUR CAMP Citric

4	**G&T:** Stimulating, which is slightly surprising given how calm the gin is when neat. There is lots of herbal, spicy activity, with an off-dry palate. Complex and persistent. Yes, good!
3	**With Sicilian Lemonade:** I expected this to sing like a Welsh choir, given the neat solo performance, but the gin hides away. A little nervous.
5	**Negroni:** N2 Floral still and almost haughty to begin with, rising above the Campari and vermouth and lying on a bed of roses. The juniper now begins to show fully and the palate slowly deepens. Balanced and showing considerable class.
4.5	**Martini:** At 4:1 you hit the ideal balance, with sufficient citrus to carry the entire length. The full complexity is calmly revealed. Excellent balance and complexity. Recommended.

BOTANICALS

Juniper • Coriander seeds • Orris root • Nutmeg • Cassia bark • Cinnamon • Liquorice root • Angelica root • Orange peel • Lemon peel

BROKER'S 47% ABV (export strength)

I'm all for fun in drinks, but I've always thought the bowler hat that sits jauntily atop the Broker's bottle makes this gin look slightly gimmicky. It was first distilled (at the Langley Distillery near Birmingham, West Midlands) in 1998 to an old recipe for brothers Martin and Andy Dawson and has been a huge success in the USA. Maybe the bowler hat helps.

It is as juniper-forward, weighty, and rootily dry as you would expect a traditional gin to be, with a crisp, almost biscuity element. Coriander, celery, violet, and spice follow on, alongside understated citrus. The palate is chewy and quite sweet with very peppery coriander surging through, closely followed by a dense cloud of juniper that opens to roots and a little nut. It's long and considerably more serious a proposition than the bottle suggests.

FLAVOUR CAMP Juniper

5*	**G&T:** Clean and dry with big gin delivery at 2:1, so you might want to lengthen it further. Perfumed on the back palate, which is so essential in this old-style G&T.
3.5	**With Sicilian Lemonade:** The gin is pretty austere and that element works against the mixer here, not allowing enough sweetness to come through.
5	**Negroni:** N1 Huge with sage, pine, and bitter herbs, and real complexity. There is a confident, well upholstered air to this with plenty of soft layers. A classic Negroni.
4	**Martini:** Dry but very up and defiant in its presence. It needs to be at 4:1 to allow the vermouth to act like a marriage guidance counsellor, calming the elements down and stopping the juniper being too bold.

BOTANICALS

Undeclared

CADENHEAD'S CLASSIC 50% ABV

Made by the independent bottling arm of J & A Mitchell, owners of the legendary Campbeltown whisky distillery Springbank, this and sister brand Old Raj (*see* p.101) have built up a cult following, particularly in the USA. This is a boldly assertive and – don't forget – strong gin with forward juniper and roots, angelica in particular. It's deep-toned, rich, and mellow, with forest-like aromas and almost gentian-like dryness. The palate is fruity with a quick bust of citrus, before it dries into a pine forest with just a touch of sweetness on the end. It's serious, yes, but importantly it's balanced. A solid performer.

FLAVOUR CAMP Juniper

4	**G&T:** Retains earthiness and power at 2:1. To be honest, it copes with any level of dilution – this is hardly a shy spirit. Good persistence, but it could be a little too dry for some.
3	**With Sicilian Lemonade:** Strangely, it becomes slightly funky when such a citric mixer is added. It's clean and has some freshness, but that juniper-root combo results in a clash.
4.5	**Negroni:** N1 Of course you still get juniper – what did you expect? Now, however, it's moved into sage and pine with a little menthol addition. There is softness behind, but this is a powerfully potent mix.
4	**Martini:** Bold and lightly vegetal. Some more sweetness emerges in time, the vermouth easing the herbal flavours forward and adding balance. It's BIG, so you've been warned.

BOTANICALS

Not fully declared but include: Juniper • Rosemary • Elderberry • Ginger • Fennel seeds

CAMBRIDGE GIN AUTUMN/ WINTER 2014 44% ABV

Will Lowe began making gin in a vacuum still in his front room. His business started out as a bespoke service where he tailored gins to suit people's preferences, but he was soon making exclusive batches for Michelin-starred restaurants. All the botanicals (which have also included wood ants for his Anty Gin) are macerated for different lengths of time and distilled separately, before being blended and married. Twice a year he and his wife Lucy, helped by their dog Darcy, forage for seasonal botanicals that go into the 50 litres (11 gallons) of Cambridge Gin. This autumn/winter release shows a fragrant piney nose with lemon meringue pie accents and distinct rosemary behind. Gently sweet and softly textured, the rich palate is very perfumed - a stroll in a herb garden with an aniseed-like hint on the tingling finish. This is best taken neat, with ice.

FLAVOUR CAMP Juniper/Herbal

2.5	**G&T:** The herbaceous elements come out immediately, but for once the tonic seems way too sweet.
2.5	**With Sicilian Lemonade:** Big, almost mossy notes and then bitter lemon. The gin is once again obliterated.
3.5	**Negroni:** N2 The herbal notes are scaled back on the nose, but the huge aromatic burst has been preserved on the palate, tempered by the vermouth; the Campari, however, is the unwanted guest.
5	**Martini:** Done at 5:1, this is clean and allows the texture to show itself. A gentle, calm release, with subtle roundness given by the vermouth and a peppery finish. Very good.

BOTANICALS

Juniper • Coriander seeds • Lemon peel • Orange peel • Angelica root • Cassia bark • Rowan berries • Coul Blush apple • Heather • Bog myrtle • Dandelion

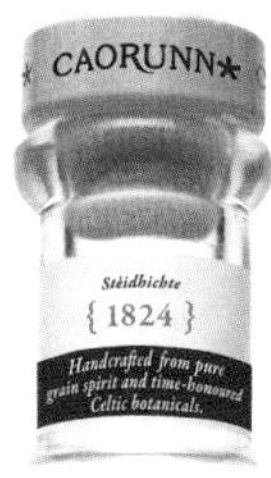

CAORUNN 41.8% ABV

Pronounced ka-roon, this relatively new Scottish gin is made at the Balmenach Distillery on the wilder edges of Speyside in the Highlands. It makes great play on its use of native Scottish botanicals – its name is Gaelic for rowan berry – which helps to root it in its immediate landscape. What is surprising is that while Balmenach is noted for its old-style, heavy whisky, Caorunn is very much a delicate New Gin.

This is very pretty to start, with apple notes, a brief hint of juniper, and then delicate florals. Though all very fresh, those higher aromatics lift away quickly, leaving a clean, lightly perfumed, lemon-accented base. Water shows the woods better. It's sweet to taste, with some texture in the centre, and is drier than the nose suggests.

FLAVOUR CAMP Floral/Fragrant	
2.5	**G&T:** Light, attractive, fresh, and fun, but just lacking in some persistence. Drink up quickly!
3	**With Sicilian Lemonade:** Even at 2:1, the mixer is too bold on the nose. It's still a pleasant drink though.
4	**Negroni:** N4. The ratio allows the perfume to lift, but the vermouth and Campari help to anchor it aromatically and give not just balance but a little weight. The bitter finish is a bonus.
3.5	**Martini:** Clean, crisp, and fresh. The lower temperature fixes the flighty botanicals, giving depth to the mid-palate. You need to have it cold and let the inside of your mouth do the work.

BOTANICALS

Juniper • Cinnamon • Nutmeg • Cassia bark • Grains of paradise • Ginger • Cumin • Clove • Coriander seeds • Angelica root • plus Elderflower and citrus infusion

DARNLEY'S VIEW 40% ABV

Made at Thames Distillers in Clapham, southwest London, for Scotch distiller/bottler Wemyss Vintage Malts, this has a slightly sharp introduction with plenty of the citrus infusion, which bumps that axis up to an intensity akin to bergamot. Then there is some cassia with moderate levels of juniper lurking behind. Water brings out a peppery edge. The palate, in contrast, is very soft, some of the floral tea element (probably the elderflower) with the roots giving a light drying grip that only then opens into marmalade-like peels. It becomes decidedly spicy towards the back.

FLAVOUR CAMP Citric/Spicy	
3.5	**G&T:** Fresh, with a fuzzy citric edge adding a soft and lightly honeyed element. Just lacks persistence.
4	**With Sicilian Lemonade:** Very up and wide-eyed, adding some weight to the lemonade while the peels fizz above.
2.5	**Negroni:** N3 Sadly, this goes a little too earthy, with the spiciness setting up a clash.
4	**Martini:** Best at 4:1, where the vermouth's floral notes form a natural link with the more aromatic elements of the gin, creating a bridge to the exuberant citrus and calming down the pepperiness, leaving it to burst through on the finish. Good.

BOTANICALS

Juniper • Angelica root • Lime peel • Bay • Black and green cardamom • Raspberry leaf • Honey

DODD'S 49.9% ABV

Distilled in Battersea, south London, this is named after Ralph Dodd, an early nineteenth-century entrepreneur, whose many schemes included the creation of The London Distillery Co. The venture failed – indeed Dodd was taken to court for his innovative notion to issue transferrable shares – but his spirit lingered on. So when the brand new London Distillery Company started producing gin in 2013, it was rightly called Dodd's. The bulk of the botanicals, including the honey, are distilled in a copper pot still, while the more delicate ones are cold distilled in a vacuum still. The two streams are then blended and married before bottling.

The nose is creamy, then a leafy shiso-like aroma emerges with fat fruits behind. In time there is subtle juniper, a menthol hit, some celery, and sweetness. The mouthfeel is very silky, which distracts you initially from the high, fresh, and brightly warm perfume. You're inside a pine forest eating a ras el hanout baklava.

FLAVOUR CAMP Juniper/Spicy

4	**G&T:** Lively, even velvety, with heavy florals. The palate starts solidly, but citrus comes through before drying into juniper. Creamy and almost medicinal.
X	**With Sicilian Lemonade:** The peels produce a candle wax note and the gin is too bold – even when lengthened.
4	**Negroni:** N1 Becomes very fruity and juicy, with massive fruits but assertive juniper. Weighty, with the gin's creaminess balancing the bitter, dark-hued edges.
5	**Martini:** The juniper is balanced against the fresh fruity elements, but it's the creamy palate that makes it a luxurious Martini. Good.

BOTANICALS

Juniper • Coriander seeds • Citrus peel • Angelica root • Orris root • plus Infused with heather and milk thistle

EDINBURGH GIN 43% ABV

Produced by Alex Nicol of the Spencerfield Spirit Company, this is a reminder to the world that at one point the Scottish capital was home to many (often illicit) gin stills, which would have been making their equivalent of Old Tom/Holland's gin (*see* p.23/p.11). He now has his own gin distillery on the Royal Mile (though this sample dates from before that).

The nose is lightly confected, estery, and fruity, with boiled sweets/bubblegum and assertive citrus. It needs time (and dilution) to show more piney elements as well as sherbet lemon. The palate is sweet with some raspberry and cherry blossom that lead into a big, broad mid-palate where herbal elements come through, before the pine and heather enter at once.

FLAVOUR CAMP Fragrant/Fruity

Score	Serve
4	**G&T:** If you like your G&T highly aromatic on the nose, then this is for you. The drier palate goes well with the tonic and is given a spicy kick. Delivers well.
4.5	**With Sicilian Lemonade:** Fruity and spicy are the key words here. This is a mix where length is important. Take it long and relaxed.
3.5	**Negroni:** N4 Resinous and slightly peppery, this makes a pretty crisp Negroni with some soft fruits in support.
4.5	**Martini:** The light fruitiness from the vermouth rounds out the delivery, while the temperature cuts back on the estery notes, allowing the presence of the palate to have a greater say. Good.

BOTANICALS

Juniper • Angelica root • Coriander seeds • Liquorice root • Grains of paradise • Lemon peel • Orange peel • Savory • plus 3 secret ones

FIFTY POUNDS GIN 43.5% ABV

The name comes from the Third Gin Act of 1736 (*see* p.17), which imposed a £50 licence on gin retailers, putting many out of business - or simply driving them underground. It's made by Charles Maxwell at Thames Distillers (*see also* pp.79, 84, 93, 105, and 166) and comes in a very heavy Hollands gin-style (*see* p.11) bottle. Like the bottle, this is clean and broad-shouldered with a light vegetal note and a nutty biscuity undertow, then the citric elements (frozen peels/lemon sorbet) take over before very sage/pine-like juniper drifts in behind. It needs time to open for Parma violet and bright spiciness to come through. The palate is fat and sweet with lots of sage and lavender as the juniper becomes more assertive. This is oily and classical.

FLAVOUR CAMP Juniper/Citric

3	**G&T:** For such a solid gin it seems to shrink away when tonic is added, with the quinine becoming a little too prominent.
5	**With Sicilian Lemonade:** Much better than the tonic, here the citric elements in the gin find a more amenable pairing. It is very refreshing.
4	**Negroni:** N2 Seems to allow the full range of aromas to show themselves, including a new thyme/herbal element along with plenty of citrus and balanced sweetness from the vermouth.
4	**Martini:** Discreet on the nose but the palate makes up for it with good weight, plenty of juniper, and decent levels of complexity. Having things wetter helps to lengthen the drink and give a slightly sweet finish. If you prefer drier, then up to 5:1.

BOTANICALS

Undeclared but include: Juniper • Coriander seeds • Lemon peel • Orange peel

FINSBURY PLATINUM 47% ABV

Made in Britain, at Langley in fact (*see* p.75), this brand was established in 1740. These days, however, it is destined solely for the German market, where it is one of the largest sellers and this very ubiquity means that it is a gin that is often overlooked. This is the premium variant bottled at a higher strength. The aromatics are quite overwhelming, not just very lemony citrus – the lead-off – but floral notes, bountiful coriander, and an earthy note. Sappy juniper is present, as is a slight steeliness that drifts towards minerality. The palate starts with a modest suggestion of a juniper base, and it becomes richer and deeper than the nose indicates. The mid-palate has that firm edginess and dry spice. Is it too rigid? We'll see.

FLAVOUR CAMP Citric

3	**G&T:** Yes, austere and flinty. It comes across like a maiden aunt who is somewhat unamused by all this nonsense.
3	**With Sicilian Lemonade:** This is pretty dry as well – even the warm, bittersweet Mediterranean influence can't melt its starchy heart.
3	**Negroni:** N2 Clean and still pretty dry. It's hard to shift it away – even the sultry attentions of the vermouth can't tempt it. All very solid and worthy.
4	**Martini:** Here, the vermouth adds the much-needed sweetness, while its herbal elements allow everything to smooth down and finally warm this icy heart. A clean and rather good Martini.

BOTANICALS

Juniper • Coriander seeds • Orris root • Angelica root • Jasmine • Cassia bark • Bitter orange peel • Lemon peel • Grapefruit peel

FORDS 45% ABV

Simon Ford was for many years the US brand ambassador for Beefeater (*see* pp.63–4) and Plymouth (*see* p.104) gins, and an industry legend. In 2013, however, he decided to give it all up to start his own spirits company, the 86 Co. Inevitably he wanted to make a gin, so began to work with Charles Maxwell at Thames Distillers (*see also* pp.79, 82, 93, 105, and 166). The first thing you notice is how well balanced it all is. Bold yes, concentrated yes, but with the botanicals seemingly lining up in a very finely tuned, ordered fashion to show themselves. The vibrant citrus comes in early on, accompanied by some rather frisky lavender-accented juniper, then cassia, before the floral heaviness of the jasmine begins to blossom and add richness. You get more drive on the palate with perky citrus as a prelude to it starting to dry pleasantly. It's very well put together.

FLAVOUR CAMP Juniper/Citric

4.5	**G&T:** More of the citrus peels are released with a very clean mid-palate and good persistence. The grapefruit adds a tingle to the finish.
4	**With Sicilian Lemonade:** This has more of a lift – which doesn't come as much of a surprise – but the key here is how the weight of the mid-palate works with the sweetness and the clean, dry finish.
4	**Negroni:** N2 Shows very clean piney/lavender juniper while the peels get to work with the vermouth and Campari. There is a lick of sweetness here that adds length and sophistication. Good gear.
5	**Martini:** Elegant with some herbal elements coming through. Clean and very up with a direct mid-palate. Very good.

BOTANICALS

Juniper • Angelica root • Cassia bark • Orris root • Coriander seeds • Clove • Cumin • Lemon peel • Orange peel • Geranium • plus 1 secret one

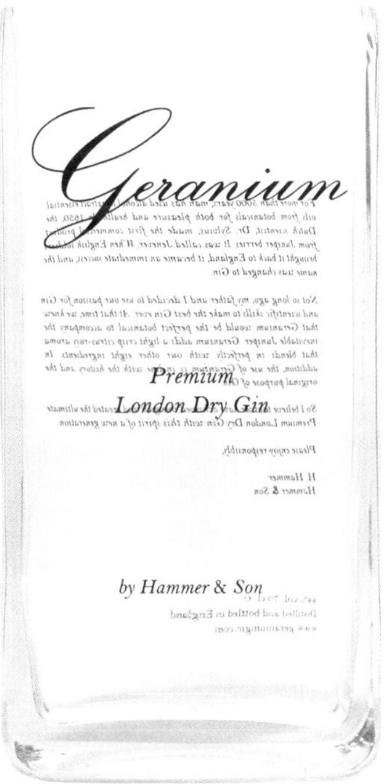

GERANIUM GIN 44% ABV

In 2009, Henrik Hammer and his father's obsessive search for a new botanical that they felt would make gin complete was revealed. Their new ingredient was geranium leaves, which is less outrageous than it sounds, as geranium shares scent molecules (particularly geraniol) with juniper and citrus. The gin is distilled at Langley Distillery (*see* p.75). Geranium appears immediately with its warm, dusty rose-citric note. It's soon backed up with lavender, pine, lemon, and just a tiny hint of clove. The key lies in the thick texture of the spirit, which helps allow the botanicals to become more rose-like. Geranium can be unforgiving, so the balance is critical – and fully achieved. The palate shows a cool freshness before the juniper muscles in along with pepper and spice.

FLAVOUR CAMP Floral

4.5	**G&T:** The perfume works well here, with the drying elements in the centre acting as a balance.
3.5	**With Sicilian Lemonade:** Needs to be lengthened – there is too much chaos at higher strength. The carbonation works, but the geranium isn't an ideal partner.
3.5	**Negroni:** N4 There is a big citric element here, along with the perfume. Velvety in feel with some rose, but it all becomes hugely floral and sweet, with a slightly confected note.
5	**Martini:** Clean and porcelain-cool in delivery. There is sufficient freshness, and the floral notes are not allowed to dominate because of the temperature. A really classy drink. In other words, keep it simple and let it speak.

BOTANICALS

Juniper • Sage • Borage • Lemon peel • Lime peel • Bitter orange peel • Coriander seeds • Angelica root

GILPIN'S 47% ABV

Produced at Thames Distillers (*see* p.79), this declares itself to be "the spirit of England". The nose is clean and quite dry with a spicy coriander freshness and woodland notes suggesting that that angelica has had a considerable part to play. This moves into a mossy note, then masses of fresh, lime-accented citrus. The juniper is light and sits next to a herbal core: that forest glade once again. It starts sweetly, then fattens out in the centre as if it's gathering breath before exhaling into sweet citrus, herbs, and spice on the back palate.

FLAVOUR CAMP Citric

3.5	**G&T:** Fresh and fragrant, and just what you want on the nose. The sage-like notes of juniper come through. Clean, but lacks a little in terms of persistence.
3.5	**With Sicilian Lemonade:** Because there is citrus already, this relates well, becoming quite subtle and tricksy with good balance. But it falls off if you don't drink it quickly, which, of course, responsible drinkers would never do.
3.5	**Negroni:** N2 The gin seems a little lost here to start, but then develops a light lavender touch on the palate, which is clean and quite crisp. Pleasantly peppery on the finish.
3.5	**Martini:** Clean; the vermouth provides the missing element that gives mid-palate oomph and links well with the angelica. Retains good character yet is more fleshed out and expressive. Drink cold to allow the heat of the mouth to release the aromas.

GORDON'S 37.5% ABV

Britain's top-selling gin, Gordon's story starts in 1769 in Bermondsey, south London, when Alexander Gordon established his first rectification plant. By 1786 he had moved to Goswell Road, Clerkenwell, where his London Dry (and many other brands) were produced until 1989, when production was moved to Laindon, Essex. Today, Gordon's is made at Diageo's Cameronbridge Distillery in Fife, Scotland. In 1992, its parent company dropped the strength to 37.5%, which not only brought it into line with its main white spirit rivals but reduced production costs and freed up money for advertising.

Light and clean with coriander spice in the lead, there are few citric elements in sight, but there is good and slightly oily juniper, with a touch of sweetness from the angelica in the background. Though rich in terms of heavy botanicals, it doesn't have great intensity yet opens nicely on the palate. The latter is light with coriander, dusty orris, and piney juniper on the end.

BOTANICALS

Undeclared but believed to include: Juniper • Coriander seeds • Angelica root • Liquorice root • Orris root • Orange peel • Lemon peel

FLAVOUR CAMP Spicy/Juniper	
2.5	**G&T:** Decent, but slightly lacking in impact from the gin (even at 2:1), making this more of a T&G rather than the other way around. The dryness of the tonic emphasizes the rootiness.
X	**With Sicilian Lemonade:** Bizarrely, this smells like baked beans and clashes badly on the tongue, adding a slightly soapy element.
3	**Negroni:** N3 It's hard to halt the advance of that coriander, but there is a little angelica peeking out from behind the vermouth and Campari. A light apéritif drink.
3	**Martini:** Slightly rooty but, as you might expect from a lower-strength gin, there is no great weight or persistence.

BOTANICALS

Undeclared but believed to include: Juniper • Coriander seeds • Angelica root • Liquorice root • Orris root • Orange peel • Lemon peel

GORDON'S EXPORT 47.3% ABV

This is the Gordon's that the rest of the world gets to enjoy – and enjoy is the word. Although this is exactly the same gin as the 37.5% (*see* p.87), this has much more in terms of top notes, with lemon peel and lime marmalade. Altogether it's much higher and brighter – it's as if the sun has been allowed to shine. Even the heavier botanicals seem to have more energy, with the roots playing a less fretful role. Coriander is now citric as well as spicy and less forceful, juniper has lavender and menthol, and there is even a hint of spent fire. It's like a different gin. While this is a resolutely old-style LDG in terms of weight and prominence of juniper, it also has lemony lift and energy; clean, mentholic, and minty. There is no comparison.

FLAVOUR CAMP Spicy/Juniper

3	**G&T:** Again, the coriander comes through most prominently and the energy seen when it's neat is dissipated.
3.5	**With Sicilian Lemonade:** More juniper comes through, which melds well with the mixer. An exciting mix – try it as a Collins perhaps (*see* p.188), though the finish is slightly short.
4	**Negroni:** N1 There is still the coriander lead, but on the palate the juniper floods through. Good balance.
3.5	**Martini:** Juniper comes out more boldly, with the vermouth allying itself with the background green herbal elements. Now there is citrus here, allowing peppery coriander to come through in the middle. A decent middle-of-the-road Martini.

BOTANICALS

Juniper • Coriander seeds • Lemon peel • Angelica root • Orris root • Liquorice root • Cassia bark • Bitter almond

GREENALL'S DRY GIN 37.5% ABV

Warrington's gin distillery in Cheshire, northwest England, was established in 1761 by Thomas Dakin (*see* p.69), whose family retained ownership for 100 years before merging and then being taken over by local brewer Greenall's (*see also* pp.65, 67, 94, and 102). It remains an important and highly respected distiller, making its own brands as well as third-party gins (including Bombay until 2014). Today, the master distiller is Joanne Moore.

This is the lower-strength version of Dakin's original 1761 recipe and is distilled in pot stills. Complexity is scaled back yet the top notes of citrus, the upper range of juniper, and the lemon peel have been retained. It's fresh and precise – the Greenall's signature. A classic, light LDG with a gingery, lime-like note. The start is a little slow, but there is a good balance, which helps drive flavour from the mid-palate onwards, with the juniper singing strongest on the finish, alongside violet and cassia.

FLAVOUR CAMP Citric/Juniper

3	**G&T:** Though this is light, it works. Sound, clean, and with character; even if low strength means a low carry, it's more than acceptable.
4	**With Sicilian Lemonade:** The mixer comes in quite strongly on the nose, but the palate has brio and verve. There's a lovely zestiness that keeps your interest.
3	**Negroni:** N2 A clean and crisp gin drink with hints of that higher-toned citrus adding to the general impression of freshness. Just lacking in penetration.
3.5	**Martini:** Becomes lightly nutty and has retained its citrus-juniper perfume while managing not to be overpowered by the vermouth.

BOTANICALS

Juniper • Coriander seeds • Nutmeg • Cinnamon • Angelica root • Orris root • Cassia bark • Liquorice root • Orange peel • Lemon peel

HAYMAN'S LONDON DRY

40% ABV

The Hayman family has been distilling gin for four generations and is today run by Christopher Hayman, his son James, and daughter Miranda. Since 2013, their gins have been made at their Witham, Essex site. The whole story speaks of tradition – as does their flagship London Dry. The look is highly polished with a silvery sheen and the nose is immediate: bold, rooty, and robust with a powerful juniper lead-off. This drifts into pine as the Parma violet/earthiness of orris and angelica (here in its celery-like guise) take charge. Pausing after this full-frontal assault you notice coriander, cassia, mace, and cinnamon, before whiffs of lime and lemon add top notes. The palate is silky and glossy with the citrus (now turned into marmalade peel), juniper, and masses of mouth-coating sweet liquorice, before juniper and drying roots come through on the finish. It's excellently balanced.

FLAVOUR CAMP Juniper	
5	**G&T:** Bold, with the tonic bringing out the angelica and liquorice, while adding a light sweetness to assist with the balance. The finish is dry, but this can be ameliorated with a lime wedge.
3.5	**With Sicilian Lemonade:** Here, it's citrus and liquorice that are promoted, then the spices with the juniper and roots stepping back.
4.5	**Negroni:** N1 Masses of juniper, the vermouth adding sweetness and depth, while the bitterness of the Campari melds with the orange peel and angelica. It's big, and serious.
4.5	**Martini:** Even at 4:1 this remains a bone-dry Martini, the vermouth adding just a subtle herbal twist. Good balance.

HAYMAN'S ROYAL DOCK

57% ABV

BOTANICALS

Juniper • Coriander seeds • Nutmeg • Cinnamon • Angelica root • Orris root • Cassia bark • Liquorice root • Orange peel • Lemon peel

Batten down the hatches mates, there's a gin storm on the way. The Hayman family pride themselves in making ultra-traditional gins and this full-blooded broadside of a naval-strength gin is no exception. Made with the standard Hayman (*see* opposite) 10 botanicals but in a different ratio, what is surprising is how the alcohol is masked and isn't overly hot. Initially, there is lemony coriander, then Yuletide memories kick in with pine, mixed peels, ginger, and coriander. Water makes it more bosky. The palate is very pure and chewy but, let's face it, needs water. It makes it thick and palate-coating, with a blast of botanicals and a whisper of Parma violet on the end.

FLAVOUR CAMP Juniper

5*	**G&T:** This needs considerable lengthening to balance. When longer, it becomes gentler with the tonic adding a little mid-palate wetness.
3.5	**With Sicilian Lemonade:** Surprisingly citric. You wonder where the gin has gone, but then it crunches in on the tongue making this mix a little too dry, the two elements working at cross-purposes.
5*	**Negroni:** N1 Would you believe, it's (almost) very well mannered, as if The Incredible Hulk still had Bruce Banner's personality, the gin managing to influence and maximize every aspect of the drink, but it's integrated.
5	**Martini:** Stir hard and long to get some dilution because this is dangerous and should be restricted to one per session. Keep it wet because the vermouth adds another layer to the mid-palate. After one of these I want to brain the splicemace!

BOTANICALS

Juniper • Angelica root • Coriander seeds • Cubeb berries • Orris root • Chamomile • Caraway seeds • Elderflower • Meadowsweet • Lemon peel • Orange peel • plus Rose and cucumber essences post-distillation

HENDRICK'S 41.4% ABV

The late Charles Grant Gordon was a whisky man (his family firm makes Glenfiddich, Balvenie, and Grant's). But, like most whisky men, he was also a gin lover and he wanted one that smelled like a picnic in an English rose garden. The result was Hendrick's. Two batches of the same botanicals (in slightly different percentages) are distilled in a Carter-Head still and a nineteenth-century Bennett pot still at their Girvan grain distillery in South Ayrshire, Scotland, then blended together, before essences of rose and cucumber are added. If this *was* a garden, then it would be one where juniper hides in the bushes, allowing light florals and green herbs to frolic on the lawn. It's the coriander seeds that dominate, bringing citric top notes and spiciness.

FLAVOUR CAMP Spicy

3	**G&T:** Becomes gentle, allowing the florals to assert themselves. It's also noticeably sweeter. Coriander takes charge in the mouth, clashing with the quinine. The roots come through on the dusty finish.
4	**With Sicilian Lemonade:** A more successful, brighter mix. The sweet nature of the gin is enhanced, while the coriander here shows its citric side. The palate is controlled, and rather than dustiness, you have spice and crispness on the end.
3.5	**Negroni:** N3 It's Campari that is the bully here, so you have to drop it (and the vermouth) down to achieve balance. Works not too badly and it's pleasant, if coriander-led.
3.5	**Martini:** The mix needs to be quite wet to give the vermouth a chance to soften things down and ally themselves with the top notes. Fine.

JENSEN'S BERMONDSEY

43% ABV

With its minimal packaging, Christian Jensen's first gin sneaked onto the market in 2004 winning many followers for its uncluttered, juniper-forward style. This was an old-style, traditional dry gin with no pretensions. For the first decade it was produced by Charles Maxwell at Thames Distillers (*see also* pp.79, 82, 84, 105, and 166) but is now produced at Jensen's distillery in Bermondsey, south London. This sample is from the latter.

This gin celebrates its juniper element. It roars with pine and sage followed by calming notes of liquorice, aniseed and violet. Only then are the coriander and peels uncaged, adding sweet spice and fleshy tangerine. Any dustiness is held in check by the oiliness of the spirit. The taste is almost discreet to start, then drives into the middle before an almond note carries it towards the finish. This is calm, ordered, precise, and complex.

BOTANICALS

Undeclared but only traditional nineteenth-century London Dry botanicals

FLAVOUR CAMP	Juniper
5*	**G&T:** A proper old-school G&T with the tonic adding effervescence, and a light drying element, while allowing the gin to come through. In time, earthy elements begin to show. Good persistence.
3.5	**With Sicilian Lemonade:** That dry earthiness is there, which makes it a little uneasy to start with, but once it gets going on the tongue, it delivers well.
5	**Negroni:** N1 Dry and juniper/root-led, and more of the Parma violet element. Big and hugely appetizing; you could eat this.
5	**Martini:** As you would expect, the juniper is to the fore, the vermouth adding a gentle supportive layer. The mid-palate is slow moving and balanced. Rich.

BOTANICALS

11 in total including: Juniper • Orange peel • Lemon peel • Coriander seeds • Liquorice root • Oak bark

LANGTONS NO.1 40% ABV

Made for Nick Dymoke-Marr and Tim Moor by Greenall's (*see also* pp.65, 67, 89, and 102), this uses water that the pair have sourced from a borehole under Skiddaw, a mountain in the Lake District, northwest England. It is a big and broad gin, but prefers to leave the juniper as a quiet contributor, leading instead with a herbal kick. Like a number of the newer gins, it has a raspberry leaf element, which gives a perception of sweetness to the nose, alongside rose and a light vegetal element like fresh spinach (which isn't unpleasant). It becomes more celery-like on the palate, with juniper and a growing citrus dimension. As things are already high-toned, the piney/rooty elements have an important role to play in slowing down some of the more excitable of the aromatics. The finish is very soft.

FLAVOUR CAMP Citric/Floral

2.5	**G&T:** It comes across to begin with as being slightly artificial, like jelly babies, then come more fruits before the ginny core reveals itself.
2.5	**With Sicilian Lemonade:** The gin is overpowered by the mixer here.
4	**Negroni:** N4 Tried it at this ratio to preserve the gin's texture and aromatics, while letting the other ingredients add to the mid-palate weight. The result is fresh and floral with some juniper, and then a juicy mid-palate. Clean and pleasing.
3.5	**Martini:** Those aromatics remain in charge, making this a fine gin for the newer gin drinker. A hint of artichoke in the mid-palate, then rose and some depth. Good clean finish.

BOTANICALS

Undeclared but include: Juniper • Coriander seeds • Lemon peel • Sweet orange peel

LONDON HILL 40% ABV

An old stager, this is made for Scotch whisky distiller/ blender Ian MacLeod at the Langley Distillery (*see* p.75) and is another that slips by unnoticed because of – well, I'm not sure precisely – the pack, the price (too low)? Whatever the reason, it's worthy of a re-examination. A medium-weight LDG mixing wintergreen-like juniper with some balsam, bright citrus peel, and a spicy coriander note, all of which work together as it moves into woodland flowers, orange peel, and angelica. The palate is soft to start and only gains energy in the middle of the tongue. Classic, old-school, juniper-accented gin. I would really like to see it at a higher strength.

FLAVOUR CAMP Juniper

3.5	**G&T:** Seems to get much brighter thanks to the carbonation. Effervescent with a slightly bitter fall-off. Dry, so it needs a lime wedge.
3.5	**With Sicilian Lemonade:** This is a sound, middle-of-the-road kind of mix, showing weight and some length, with attractive top notes developing. I'd probably rather use it for a Fizz.
3.5	**Negroni:** N1 Quite restrained and gentle with plenty of resonant deep notes. Holds well on the palate, lightening and becoming more citric and pleasingly bitter on the end.
4.5	**Martini:** The transformation is remarkable, as if the other mixes are slightly beneath it. Now, as a Martini, it puts on its dinner jacket, polishes its cufflinks, and becomes this rather debonair gentleman. Crisp and beautifully presented.

BOTANICALS

Juniper • Liquorice root • Orris root • Cinnamon • Almond • Savory • Coriander seeds • Angelica root • Cassia bark • Lemon peel • Orange peel • plus Infusion with bergamot and gardenia flowers

THE LONDON NO.1 47% ABV

Made at Thames Distillers (*see* p.79) for sherry house Gonzalez Byass, this starts life as a pretty classic LDG, but has a long maceration with gardenia flowers that turns the whole shebang blue. The gin is a little shy to start – surprisingly given the strength – and is made in a herbal style. It's quite discreet with orange peel and bergamot prominent, then delicate juniper, eucalyptus, and wild thyme; if anything, it points to Spanish gin rather than back to London. The palate is crisp and tighter than expected, lightly peppery with fruit blossom.

FLAVOUR CAMP Citric/Herbal

5	**G&T:** Significantly enhanced by the tonic, this is an exuberant and exotic mix. It can be lengthened, but I'd keep things Spanish and have it harder.
3.5	**With Sicilian Lemonade:** The mixer dominates proceedings on the nose, but the palate comes to the rescue where a certain unity is achieved. A grown-up soft drink.
3.5	**Negroni:** N2 A slightly muted nose with a fleshy palate. Big and sweet, with some brio and style.
4	**Martini:** OK, it's blue, but drink it in the dark if that offends you. Softer and sweet, with the bergamot being very prominent along with some juniper. Controlled and pleasant.

BOTANICALS

Juniper • Coriander seeds • Angelica root • Orris root • Liquorice root • Cassia bark • Lime peel • Lemon peel • Orange peel • plus Cucumber essence added post-distillation

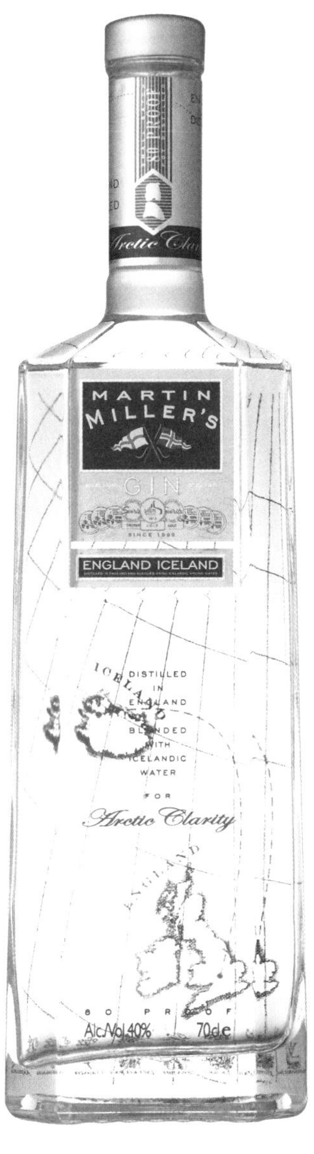

MARTIN MILLER'S 40% ABV

When this arrived in 1999, most gin lovers wondered quite what the late Martin Miller was playing at with his use of Icelandic water and cucumber essence. Little did we know that practices such as these would become the norm. New Gin was very much here to stay.

It remains a 10-strong botanical mix, distilled by Langley (*see* p.75) in two batches: roots and spices, followed by citrus, before being blended with the cucumber, then shipped to Iceland for dilution with glacier water. It has a citric lead-off: lime, orange pips, tangerine, lemon, and light (and also citric) coriander, behind all of which is some resinous juniper. It's all quite lively, but maintains its persistence over time. The palate is quite sweet and slightly waxy. The drying element starts quite quickly on the tongue, although the citrus persists aromatically, while the finish brings out the waxed fruit element.

FLAVOUR CAMP Citric

4	**G&T:** Well, there is no need to wonder what citrus peel to use here. None. Amazingly fresh and vibrant, and though that initial burst fades, it has drive.
4	**With Sicilian Lemonade:** What's weird is how a citric mixer also brings out the rooty elements, while squeezing out a little sweetness in the centre.
3.5	**Negroni:** N2 Citrus remains the main player here, but without any waxiness. Well balanced palate with Seville orange, but a bittersweet edge just tips things into slight astringency.
4	**Martini:** Fresh and very waxy. The addition of vermouth acts as a trigger for the more aromatic top notes, making it more perfumed. It has decent lift.

BOTANICALS

Juniper • Coriander seeds • Angelica root • Orris root • Lemon peel • Orange peel • Cassia bark • Lime peel • Nutmeg • Cinnamon • plus Cucumber essence added post-distillation

MARTIN MILLER'S WESTBOURNE STRENGTH

45.2% ABV

Named after Martin Miller's original office in Westbourne Grove, Notting Hill, west London, it's fascinating to see the difference between this and the original (*see* p.97). The strength is higher, and while the botanical mix remains the same, the percentages are different. The result is a gin that is broader in character. The citric burst that defines its brother is calmer here, allowing better equilibrium between all of the botanicals – there seems to be more angelica coming through. It's fatter and almost autumnal, whereas the original is definitely spring. Thick and lightly vegetal, it has bolder lemon accents and more prominent juniper on the palate. The signature waxiness is retained but has been calmed. It's zesty on the finish and shows good integration.

FLAVOUR CAMP Citric/Juniper

4	**G&T:** At 2:1, it shows its alcoholic seriousness. Very lightly confected when mixed, but a solid and quite dry mid-palate with enough citrus to stop the quinine attaching itself to the roots and dragging everything down. Good persistence.
3	**With Sicilian Lemonade:** Brings out a slightly stewed aroma to start and the waxiness is also accentuated as the citric elements bind together. A decent enough mix.
3.5	**Negroni:** N2 It remains waxy with a little sage element coming through, the vermouth adding some bruised fruits. Balanced and quite dry.
4.5	**Martini:** Very citric and elegant – the alcohol helps in this setting, with the vermouth as a background. Mid-palate weight is good and the wax has turned to a viscous oiliness.

BOTANICALS

Juniper • Cassia bark • Coriander seeds • Angelica root • Clove • Cumin

MOMBASA CLUB 41.5% ABV

We have Old Raj (*see* p.101), so I suppose it's inevitable that there should be another gin that harks back to the days of the British Empire. This is it, made by Thames Distillers (*see* p.79) with a botanical mix oriented towards spiciness (appropriate enough given Mombasa's position opposite the Spice Island of Zanzibar). The nose is dry with lots of nut oil, a big blast of earthy lemony cumin, clove galore, and nutmeg. It's a bit like an alcoholic garam masala. The palate is soft and, yes, spicy with a dryness to the centre, which then opens pleasantly to finally show lavender-like juniper, violet, black pepper, and nutmeg.

FLAVOUR CAMP Spicy

3	**G&T:** It gets pretty funky and interesting here, like post-coital skin. You feel kind of voyeuristic just smelling it, but the lack of top notes brings it down, and a squeeze of citrus helps.
5	**With Sicilian Lemonade:** If you want top notes, this provides them, which allow the lemony elements in coriander and cumin to show. Try as a Collins as well (*see* p.188), as this mix really does work.
3.5	**Negroni:** N2 The spiciness might be the dominant feature here, but it's so powerful that the vermouth needs to be upped to achieve a balance. Once that happens, you get this slightly restless twitching drink that's actually quite fun.
3.5	**Martini:** Now everything becomes rather Christmassy, which is no bad thing – this might work in a Warm Gin Punch (*see* p.190). At this point, though, we have a mulled Martini, which is kinda weird. Better as a Martinez.

BOTANICALS

Juniper • Coriander seeds • Orris root • Grapefruit peel • Orange peel • Cardamom

NO.3 46% ABV

The venerable London wine and spirit merchant Berry Bros. & Rudd has been trading from 3, St James's Street since 1698 and was supplying the gentry of the capital when its unwashed were sluicing back Mother's Ruin. It moved into the premium sector in 2010 with the launch of No.3.

Designed by Dr. David Clutton and distilled in Holland, it nods both to gin history with the simplicity of its botanical recipe and to the present day with the inclusion of grapefruit. The nose is elegant and rich, with the warm menthol notes of cardamom drifting over, before the juniper's pine and lavender notes are released. Just as it seems to be moving inexorably down towards the roots, in comes the grapefruit and orange and coriander to give it brightness. In time, the peels take the forward position, while water brings out a pleasing dustiness from the orris. The palate is polished and smooth.

FLAVOUR CAMP Spicy/Juniper

4	**G&T:** Back comes that cardamom. Quite fragrant now, then it dives deep into juniper. This has persistence and good length.
3	**With Sicilian Lemonade:** There is a bit of a clash here, with the bitter peels from the lemonade and the cardamom from the gin not exactly rubbing along together.
5	**Negroni:** N2 The grapefruit is the secret weapon here as it provides the cut-through while the juniper and cardamom buddy up with the vermouth. Campari integrates well, adding its own little fiercely sweet darts. A very urbane drink.
5*	**Martini:** At its best here. Exotic with all the elements in harmony, you also get an idea of its richness and weight, with just enough sweetness allied to the vermouth to carry.

BOTANICALS

Juniper • Coriander seeds • Angelica root • Orris root • Cassia bark • Almond • Lemon peel • Orange peel • plus Coloured with saffron post-distillation

OLD RAJ 55% ABV

A legendary, nay, cult, gin, Old Raj is made at the Springbank whisky distillery in Campbeltown, in Kintyre, Scotland. Its most notable claim to fame is the use of a small amount of saffron post-distillation, giving it a light lemony hue. Even at this high strength it is more subtle aromatically than its sister brand Cadenhead Classic (*see* p.76), with pine and citrus predominating. While undoubtedly dry, there is a little twist of herbs, a tickle of menthol, a little floral lift, and the deep softness of saffron and almond. The feel is thick and viscous with big juniper to start before a fizzing citric burst, then balanced roots. The alcohol adds a certain edge to the proceedings. It's reliably old style. What did you expect?

FLAVOUR CAMP Juniper/Citric	
4.5	**G&T:** Good citric, aromatic lift, and, thanks to the high strength, fair persistence as well. It's clean, it's long. In short, it works.
5*	**With Sicilian Lemonade:** The pine and high citric elements meld together. A fragrant element emerges on the palate. One of those drinks where the sum is greater than the parts.
4	**Negroni:** N1 The gin is clean with a light honeyed aspect to it from the base spirit. The mix helps to bring the citrus forwards, with the juniper and roots sinking back into the plump cushion of vermouth.
5*	**Martini:** Slightly fat at 4:1, as the vermouth allows more of the herbal side to come through, but you need this a little wetter because of the strength. Elegant with real personality.

BOTANICALS

Undeclared but include: Juniper • Coriander seeds • Angelica root • Cubeb berries • Cardamom • Ginger • Black pepper • Orange peel • Lemon peel • Grapefruit peel

OPIHR 40% ABV

A spiced gin made by Greenall's (*see also* pp.65, 67, 89, and 94) that smells like a takeaway curry – that mix of peppercorn, cubeb, cumin, coriander, curry leaf, turmeric, and fenugreek. You can imagine crunching on the free poppadums. It's hard to see quite where the juniper is hiding. Less hot and peppery on the palate to start, it lulls you into a false sense of security, because then the spices come frolicking out. It's all a little bit odd to be honest, but kind of compelling, as these things often are.

FLAVOUR CAMP Spicy (and then some)

4.5	**G&T:** I wasn't expecting this to work – the gin is too bold, the juniper well hidden, but it does. Shut your eyes, think Indian restaurant, think a drink you need to have with curry, and this is it. But is it a G&T? I think it's something else, but it's good.
X	**With Sicilian Lemonade:** Afraid not. The sweetness comes across as being awkward, and the fierce spiciness ends up creating a bitter clash.
4	**Negroni:** N1 All the cardamom comes through alongside pepper and ginger, but on the palate everything comes together with the spices only sneaking through fully on the end. A lot of fun.
2.5	**Martini:** As you might have gathered, this is not a gin that can be suppressed or shifted into a new shape, and while the temperature slows the heat of the spices, the palate is a mess.

BOTANICALS

Juniper • Coriander seeds • Angelica root • Liquorice root • Vanilla • Meadowsweet • Fresh grapefruit peel • Fresh lemon peel • Fresh orange peel • Cocoa nibs • Cassia bark • Grains of paradise • Nutmeg • Orris root

OXLEY 47% ABV

This started as an experiment by Bacardi (owner of Bombay Sapphire, *see* p.70) to distil at low temperatures (under vacuum) to avoid cooked compounds coming through. It is made for them at a special unit within Thames Distillers (*see* p.79). All of the 14 botanicals are batched individually, vacuum-sealed, and frozen to retain their intensity. They are then distilled together.

The nose has a fennel-like top note, some liquorice, intense Seville orange, and tangerine, before spices emerge along with low juniper. Water makes it bigger and almost off-dry, while on the palate you get the sensation of the botanicals slowly popping on your tongue. It becomes quite aromatic and peppery on the long, clean finish, with a little menthol, mace, light liquorice sweetness, and juniper. Water makes it more exotic. Best sipped cold, neat, and with ice.

FLAVOUR CAMP Citric/Spicy

3.5	**G&T:** More grapefruit, and a clean and crisp delivery. Remains quite light, so have it short and drink it quickly.
3	**With Sicilian Lemonade:** The bitter lemon slightly swamps the gin, but the mid-palate where the dry, the sweet, and the bitter all meet is interesting. Again, have it short and sharp – Fizz style.
3.5	**Negroni:** N2 The delicacy of the gin necessitates a lighter ratio – in fact, I'd replace the Campari with Aperol – but even then there is too much going on to get a proper balance.
3.5	**Martini:** Take it to 5:1 and it becomes crisply turned out. It remains delicate, making me wonder if this is the classic breakfast Martini, or whether that's just irresponsible.

BOTANICALS

Juniper • Coriander seeds • Lemon peel • Sweet orange peel • Angelica root • Orris root • Cardamom

PLYMOUTH GIN 41.2% ABV

Mr Coates opened his Black Friars distillery in 1793, looking to make a higher-class spirit, and by the middle of the nineteenth century was supplying over 1,000 casks of Navy Strength a year to the British Navy. But by the 1980s, Plymouth Gin's glory days were long gone. Uninterested owners had cut its strength and changed the recipe. Yet in 1996, Charles Rolls (now of Fever-Tree) bought the brand, upped the strength, and restored the old recipe. Plymouth was back. It is now part of Chivas Brothers, owned by Pernod Ricard.

Soft, heathery juniper leads off, along with some citrus, before moving into menthol, sage, and delicate sweetness. Balanced and calm on the tongue, with a sense of botanicals being laid down in layers rather than stretching out along the tongue's length. It then becomes more piney, with citrus balancing. A slow swell of violet and very gentle roots round it off.

FLAVOUR CAMP Juniper	
4.5	**G&T:** Good juniper persistence; quite light and balanced. It works with the tonic and has some length.
4.5	**With Sicilian Lemonade:** That sweet citrus and the lemon in perfect accord. Lifted and fresh.
5	**Negroni:** N1 The orange is the key here and is brought forward by the other ingredients. Complex and decadent, with a silky, sexy delivery.
5*	**Martini:** The vermouth brings in hedgerow notes to the complex mix and the oily texture is thickened, making this a very sensual Martini. Great personality, gentle, and long.

BOTANICALS

Juniper • Lemon peel • Bitter orange peel • Coriander seeds • Orris root • Angelica root • Cassia bark • Liquorice root • Nutmeg

PORTOBELLO ROAD NO. 171

42% ABV

This gin was created by London bartending legend Jake Burger along with his business partner Ged Feltham, and is made to their specifications by gin-distilling maestro Charles Maxwell at Thames Distillers (*see also* pp.79, 82, 84, 93, and 166). It's clean and spicy, with a lead-off of nutmeg and cassia coming across over discreet (but evident) mentholic juniper and coriander. A light leafy green element develops from the angelica. Complex and cunning, it needs time to develop and comes to life when diluted, with more peel, violet, and cinnamon. The palate is clean, tongue-clinging, and lightly oily with every element well bedded in – a touch of juniper, a light jab of citrus, a grind of spice, and plenty of cassia and nutmeg on the end. Jake and Ged also run London Ginstitute above their bar, The Portobello Star, at 171 Portobello Road, Notting Hill.

FLAVOUR CAMP Spicy/Juniper	
3.5	**G&T:** Subtle and clean, the G&T retains character and persistence, although the finish can be a little abrupt if you forget to add citrus.
4	**With Sicilian Lemonade:** Much better than the G&T, this has lift, allowing the gin to blossom and not dwell on the darker bitter elements of life.
5	**Negroni:** N2 This is a big Negroni, with weight and succulence. The vermouth just adds a sense of control as the spices, juniper, and Campari romp around.
5	**Martini:** As you might expect from a bartender's gin, this is one made for cocktails and the Martini is where it truly delivers. Clean, assertive, layered, and, while it's bold, it is never overpowering. Its balance is seen at its best here.

BOTANICALS

12 in total including: Juniper • Cardamom • Nutmeg • Frankincense

SACRED GIN 40% ABV

Ian Hart is a revolutionary. He showed how it was possible to make world-class gins in the (relative) comfort of your home. Since 2009, he has been distilling individual botanicals in a vacuum still and then blending them into an ever-expanding range.

This is his benchmark brand, which, among a further 11 botanicals, uses frankincense, whose Latin name *Boswellia sacra* gives the distillery its name. The nose is restrained and elegant with good equilibrium between different elements. Fresh citrus is the dominant note, while the juniper remains low. It's subtle and poised, making you wonder whether anything can, or should, disturb such excellent balance. On the palate the flavours remain precise and subtle, with the frankincense's warm resinous depth making itself noticed alongside light lavender, sharply fresh citrus, and warm sweet spice. Although it has some verve, it's like Audrey Hepburn tapping her foot. Calm is the word.

FLAVOUR CAMP Citric/Spicy

3.5	**G&T:** Frankincense definitely and more citrus. It has good mouthfeel - this is a palate gin - but no great persistence.
3	**With Sicilian Lemonade:** Very subtle and quite gentle and, as suspected, there is not enough to cut through.
5*	**Negroni:** N2 The aromatics come across well with an added exotic edge to them along with a touch of mint. A perfumed mellow palate. Complex and not at all diffident. Class shows.
4.5	**Martini:** It works and works well, but only when you scale down the vermouth to a 6:1 ratio, allowing this very subtle gin to show its wares. Good complexity.

BOTANICALS

Juniper • Coriander seeds • Angelica root • Liquorice root • Orris root • Almond • Cassia bark • Cinnamon • Seville orange peel • Lemon peel

SIPSMITH 41.6% ABV

Sam Galsworthy and Fairfax Hall came into the world of gin in 2009, just as its revival was beginning to pick up pace but before there were 1,001 new brands – in other words, at precisely the right time. With no experience of distilling, they hired cocktail historian Jared Brown as consultant (now master distiller), converted a garage in Fulham, southwest London, and got started. The fact that they have now built a larger distillery shows how well they have surfed gin's latest wave.

With a historian at the helm, Sipsmith was never going to be a New Gin, but one that had a weather eye on the past while revelling in the ability to experiment. This is traditional LDG, big with a slightly earthy, pine forest/cone nose that also throws in lilac and curried spices, and a palate where complex green notes merge with those on the nose. It's generous, gentle, and slightly creamy.

FLAVOUR CAMP Juniper

4	**G&T:** As you might expect, this is assertive, rich, and long-lasting. Quinine is balanced and there is just enough fizz to make it interesting.
4.5	**With Sicilian Lemonade:** Between the two mixers, this is the one I prefer because of the way in which the citrus adds another dimension and a further layer of complexity.
5	**Negroni:** N1 Balanced and rich, with positive juniper that has now been subtly sweetened. The violet persists and there is an added dark liquorice kiss-off.
5	**Martini:** The vermouth adds an almost honeyed, vinous note to the middle, which results in a little tweak of breadth and aromatic lift. Deep and layered.

BOTANICALS

Juniper • Coriander seeds • Angelica root • Liquorice root • Orris root • Almond • Cassia bark • Cinnamon • Seville orange peel • Lemon peel

SIPSMITH V.J.O.P. 57.7% ABV

The idea of V.J.O.P. – Very Junipery Over Proof Gin – came to Jared Brown when he was musing on how predominant you can make juniper without producing something that smells of turpentine. His cunning solution was to add the juniper in three ways: macerated, just prior to distillation, and finally with some in a botanical basket. Doing this allowed him to extract different notes from the same ingredient.

It's like being lost in a Christmas tree plantation while hearing the sounds of approaching chainsaws, resulting in you pushing ever harder against the resinous needles. There is a lovely medicinal edge, some cigar/cedar, sage, and lavender. The palate is dry with orange adding lift, before it softens into almond and coriander seeds. This is not a gin for the faint-hearted or those who like things on the perfumed side.

FLAVOUR CAMP Juniper

5*	**G&T:** Big. Sorry, BIG. Here the juniper unfolds itself from the chair in which it has been lounging and whacks you in the face. There is a smarting citrus element as well.
3.5	**With Sicilian Lemonade:** Still that huge character, although here it rather overdominates. Too dry.
5*	**Negroni:** N1 Here the juniper is enfolded into the drink, allowing berry fruits (think black cherry) to emerge along with bittersweet bursts. Huge, dark, menacing, and delicious.
5	**Martini:** There is actually something slightly ridiculous about how massive this gin is and the mix needs to be fairly wet just to calm down the sheer exuberance. Savoury, with the herbs weaving in and out of the mix. Insanely strong.

BOTANICALS

Juniper • Coriander seeds • Orris root • Cardamom • Almond • Cinnamon • Liquorice root • Sweet orange peel • Lemon peel • Grapefruit peel • Devon violet

TARQUIN'S 42% ABV

Made in tiny batches in a tiny still by Tarquin Leadbetter in St Ervan, Cornwall (he also came up with the frankly genius idea of making Cornish pastis), this is another New Gin that is making friends quickly. Dry, citric, and almost floral in the (well mannered) attack, there is a violet-root element behind some lemon, a menthol hit from cardamom, and sweet liquorice. In other words, balance has been achieved. Some roasted spice is also discernible when the glass reaches the lips. The palate is soft and, while not exactly energetic, has a gentle medium weight to it that opens into forest notes and almond. A very classy new arrival.

FLAVOUR CAMP Citric/Juniper

3.5	**G&T:** Big and clean with sound juniper/quinine working together, but maybe loses impact as the gin is so soft in the centre. Decent persistence.
3.5	**With Sicilian Lemonade:** Clean and bittersweet (which is what you want), with that zestier delivery helping to give things a kick. It slightly falls away at the end.
5	**Negroni:** N2 This ratio allows the top notes to come through, the violet to link with the vermouth, and the juniper to bed down into the dark red fruits. Fleshy with great integration. It has life and balance.
4.5	**Martini:** Clean and quite elegant. A late afternoon/early evening drink, all very polite and whistle clean. Crisp with slow-drying and lively top notes. Best at 4:1.

BOTANICALS

Juniper • Angelica root • Coriander seeds • Liquorice root

TANQUERAY LONDON DRY GIN

43.1% ABV

Charles Tanqueray established his business in London's Bloomsbury in 1830 when the district was noted for its waters rather than its literary pretensions. It remains typical of its time in the simplicity of its botanical mix; its top notes are provided by the higher tones of coriander and juniper.

One of the great names in gin, these days it's made at Diageo's Cameronbridge Distillery (*see* p.87), but it still uses the Old Tom still (*see* p.23) that sat in its old site. Tanqueray is bone dry and direct, with massive piney juniper/coriander to start. Here everything has its own presence while supporting the other botanicals – a triumph of simplicity. It's slightly dusty to start, needing time for the purple cloud of juniper to spread. Think of a distilled fir tree and you'll not be far off the mark. Austere, it's for classicists, not modernists.

FLAVOUR CAMP Juniper

4	**G&T:** A boldly assertive mix, so stretch out to 1:3 or more. The dryness also makes the quinine more apparent. It's balanced, but not for the faint-hearted.
4.5	**With Sicilian Lemonade:** I was expecting a clash here, but it's surprisingly well behaved, adding a subtle, angular citric element.
5	**Negroni:** N1 Rumbustious, rich, and deep, there can be no suppressing the powerful piney notes of the gin, which are made more exotic by vermouth while Campari adds a bitter, citric edge. Serious gear.
5*	**Martini:** Tanqueray is made for this. The vermouth becomes a major contributor, adding lift while the oiliness of the gin comes through. Don't mess with Tanqueray – this is how it's meant to be drunk.

BOTANICALS

Juniper • Angelica root • Coriander seeds • Liquorice root • Chamomile flowers • Fresh orange peel • Fresh lime • Fresh grapefruit peel

TANQUERAY NO. TEN 47.3% ABV

Launched in 2000 as a range extension, this claims to be the first gin to use fresh rather than dried peels. These are first distilled in the Tiny Ten still before the spirit is added to the main Tanqueray pot still along with the other botanicals.

Though the base is the same, this is miles away from the earthy, juniper-laden power of standard Tanqueray (*see* opposite). The impression is of a slightly confused bachelor lost in a seraglio: there are masses of fresh citrus, more green angelica, still some pine, almost cedar/yew notes, and sandalwood incense. The palate is fleshy with heavy florals and fruit-syrup inference, but the pine is still there. Everything is well controlled. It remains A Gin.

FLAVOUR CAMP Citric

2	**G&T:** The fruits and the tonic clash, and the bubbles seem to fragment things rather than making them cohere. Becomes almost soapy.
3.5	**With Sicilian Lemonade:** Better and more amenable with the fruits all binding together. It's light, it's fresh, and it's, yes, fruity.
5	**Negroni:** N2 Aromatic. The scaling back of the other two ingredients produces a new rose-like aroma alongside the citrus, fruit, and pine. A clean and fresh afternoon Negroni with a funky herbal finish.
5*	**Martini:** It's made for this serve. If you like fragrance, go for the slightly wetter 4:1, which makes it luxurious. Personally, I'd go out to 5:1, where the juniper is in better balance.

BOTANICALS

Juniper • Angelica root • Coriander seeds • Liquorice root • Ginger • Bay • Rangpur lime

TANQUERAY RANGPUR 41.3% ABV

Made in 2009, here we have the standard recipe (*see* p.110) plus Rangpur limes. And it is, well, limey. Very limey. As limey as if Mr Harry Lime slid down a lime tree wearing a suit made of limes. The citric elements on the nose almost put the whole ensemble into the realms of bath oil, though there is some nuttiness in there. The peels have added not just aroma but a slight bitterness, and there seems to be a bit of sugar added to counter this. If you like limes, you'll like this. But if you don't...

FLAVOUR CAMP Citric	
2	**G&T:** Nothing can curb the lime aroma and taste, but the quinine makes it hard and bitter.
3	**With Sicilian Lemonade:** Slightly better, but even at high levels of dilution there is a bitterness.
3	**Negroni:** N2 The vermouth in particular has softened the aggressive lime, giving the sweetness of the gin an ally, while the nature of the Campari offers... interesting... top notes. It needs careful handling, but there is a germ of an idea in here.
3	**Martini:** I'd have it naked. When you do, it's OK. If you like Gimlets, that is.

BOTANICALS

Undeclared but known to include:
Juniper • Orris root • Angelica root • Citrus peels

TWO BIRDS 40% ABV

Made in 100-bottle batches by Mark Gamble in a 25-litre (5½-gallon) copper still in Market Harborough, Leicestershire, this is a relatively new gin on the market, beginning operations in 2012. Although contemporary in look, one sniff reveals that it's quite definitely – defiantly even – old style in expressiveness. It starts high-toned in that bright, intense, lemon-accented fashion, but here there is also lemon balm, and juniper in its terpene-rich element; all explosively fresh and clean. For a second you wonder if this might just be bluster, but it delivers on the palate where it's softer than the nose suggests, adding a heathland's worth of juniper and powerful penetrating pine, before some light violet and citrus come through. Gamble is also now innovating with various different casks for new variants. This is a brand to watch out for.

FLAVOUR CAMP Juniper

4.5	**G&T:** A great mix with plenty of contrasting elements: dry, sweet, spicy, citric, and bitter all dancing around each other like they are at a school disco. Intensely aromatic.
2.5	**With Sicilian Lemonade:** That intensity is almost too much and even when lengthened there is a clash taking place.
5	**Negroni:** N1 Clean and serious with fine melding of all the components. The juniper is now better controlled and there is a new dark element rumbling away. A thinking person's Negroni and an impressive debut.
4	**Martini:** As expected. Even chilling it down doesn't do much to suppress its energy. At the start the juniper ignites into action before the vermouth tries to put some sort of brake on proceedings. The finish becomes lightly perfumed. Good.

BOTANICALS

Include: Juniper • Coriander seeds • Angelica root • Lavender • Cardamom • Black pepper • Cinnamon • Elderflower • Orange peel

WARNER EDWARDS HARRINGTON DRY 44% ABV

This is distilled in Harrington, Northamptonshire, by Tom Warner and Sion Edwards, who met each other at agricultural college and then, post-graduation, decided to work together. They started with the production of essential oils but, inevitably, ended up with gin. Edwards farms in Wales, Warner at Harrington, and some of the botanicals used are sourced from their respective properties. One of the main ones is elderflower and there is a huge tisane note that comes across early on, followed by soft fruits and the start of pine, lavender, and warm spices. Showing real complexity, the delivery is slow and unctuous in character with the soporific effects of flowers. A drowsy summer afternoon of a gin, with sharp jags of citrus keeping you awake, it's textured and really well made.

FLAVOUR CAMP Juniper/Floral

3.5	**G&T:** At 2:1 there is still a big gin influence, so take it further out to where the effervescence can work more effectively and allow the drier elements to be teased out.
5	**With Sicilian Lemonade:** This works much better; the lemon and the flowers make a lovely match and it brightens up in the mouth. Also makes an excellent Collins (*see* p.188).
4	**Negroni:** N2 The elderflower has been retained with upbeat Campari and the vermouth emerging stealthily. Layered on the palate, then Seville orange peel. Good.
5	**Martini:** A little too fat at 4:1, so dry it a little to be able to see the gin. The vermouth is naturally allied with the top notes, but at 5:1 you have a crisper, flintier Martini without losing any complexity. Very good.

BOTANICALS

Juniper • Coriander seeds • Baobab fruit • Cape gooseberry (physalis) • Lemon peel • Sweet orange peel • Angelica root • Orris root • Cassia bark

WHITLEY NEILL 42% ABV

As Johnny Neill is an eighth-generation member of the Greenall Whitley distilling family (*see also* pp.65, 67, 89, 94, and 102), it was inevitable that he would create his own brand. The question was what would set it apart. The solution came via his African-born wife. Instead of sticking with the standard citrus, why not use the fruits of the baobab tree and Cape gooseberry to sit alongside a classic LDG base? The gin is distilled to his specification by Langley (*see* p.75).

The nose shows bittersweet vibrancy, with fruity notes, soft coriander, and pine trees behind, then zesty grapefruit, lemon, and a hint of florals. It's well balanced with good weight and lightly exotic. The palate is energetic and dry with coriander-seed huskiness coming through, preceded by ginger, a fruity citrus blast, and big pine cone–juniper accents, before sweet earthiness finishes things off.

FLAVOUR CAMP Citric/Juniper

4	**G&T:** It comes alive. Those citric top notes are given a boost, the juniper plays in the mid-ground, and the finish is extended. Zesty and spicy.
3.5	**With Sicilian Lemonade:** The mixer is a little too bold to see the gin in clear profile, but it's refreshing. Again, a little sweetness has helped.
3.5	**Negroni:** N2 There is a cacao-like element in here that holds the base line of the drink, allowing the top notes to lift off and add a zesty bite. Subtle tropical fruitiness then develops. A sound Negroni.
4	**Martini:** If you like the whole grapefruit/spice thing – and coriander – this is the ideal Martini gin for you. Dry but clearly a gin drink, which can only be A Good Thing.

BOTANICALS

Juniper • Coriander seeds • Angelica seeds and root • Liquorice root • Orris root • Orange peel • Lemon peel • Hops • Elderflower • Bramley apple

WILLIAMS CHASE ELEGANT CRISP GIN 48% ABV

The Chase Distillery in Herefordshire started off making potato vodka (William Chase was a potato farmer and crisp magnate) and then branched into gin. Rather than being potato-based, this uses apple spirit and that's what comes across to start with, alongside some intense hoppiness. There are fragrant, lightly floral top notes and it's very New Gin in style, with low juniper and coriander in its lemony guise. The effect is to make the gin seem not too dry, but that will change. The palate is upfront and citric but, as the name suggests, becomes dry. Now there is more coriander and celery-like angelica, with the apple coming through – almost like cider vinegar – again on the finish.

FLAVOUR CAMP Fragrant

3.5	**G&T:** The same initial lead-off is here as well with some floral notes behind. Clean and pretty dry, and a little austere on the finish, though lengthening helps.
3	**With Sicilian Lemonade:** The two orchards seem to be fighting each other here on the nose, but reach a truce on the palate, though it's short-lived, as the dryness of the gin closes it down.
2.5	**Negroni:** N2 The hop/sour apple element is still prominent. Becomes very fruity on the middle, but then fragments.
3	**Martini:** If you keep it wet, then you can balance the vinegar crispness of the gin with the softer side of the vermouth, which helps flesh out the body.

CONTINENTAL & REST OF THE WORLD

Gin was born in continental Europe, but its story has slowly become one dominated by English brands. That situation is now righting itself. Besides a renewed interest in genever (which comes later, fear not), distillers across the world are either reviving old styles or creating new gins that reflect their place of birth.

It's no surprise that Spain, the cradle of the new G&T, has a healthy representation here and that its gins have their own distinctive styles. The Dutch and Belgian approach to dry gin is as much influenced by their centuries-long experience with genever as it is with English gins. German-speaking Europe is also weighing in with its own gins – again grounded on the principle of a spirit that has been influenced by native botanicals. This is clearly seen in the new French gins, where botanicals and base spirit are used to craft gins that are not only an expression of their locality but take the category forward.

There are gins from the new small distillers in Scandinavia, whose food culture, in which juniper is so prominent, has acted as a creative trigger. The alliance of the local with the global that has always been one of gin's mainstays also manifests itself in gins from Australia, South Africa, and Canada.

Gin has always distilled the world. Now it's distilled across the world.

BOTANICALS

Juniper • Almond • Orris root • Fennel seeds • Aniseed • Grains of paradise • Orange peel • Cardamom • Violet root • Lemon peel • Coriander seeds • Cubeb berries • Cassia bark • Liquorice root • Savory • Nutmeg • Angelica root • Cumin • Cinnamon

CITADELLE 44% ABV France

While France night not be the first country you think of when gin is mentioned, it has been produced there for centuries. French gin made in Dunkirk was smuggled into England at the end of the eighteenth century (*see* p.20). It was a high point of sorts, and by the twentieth century the tradition had all but died out. Enter Alexandre Gabriel of Cognac producer Pierre Ferrand who, in 1989, decided to revive the production of "Dunkirk-style" dry gin. The result was Citadelle. Clean, fragrant, and almost ethereal to start, the complexity soon builds with pine, cassia, cardamom, and peels, all held in check by the floral element. The palate shows aniseed, orange peel, and more of a herbal element; lifted, complex, and graceful.

FLAVOUR CAMP Floral/Fragrant

5*	**G&T:** G&Ts can be a little harsh, but here the tonic enhances the top notes, while the palate shows some mint, fennel, camphor, and juniper. Subtle and aromatic.
2.5	**With Sicilian Lemonade:** Here, though, the gin and the lemon end up in an unseemly scrap.
5	**Negroni:** N2 One of the few gins that worked with any ratio of vermouth and any vermouth brand, showing how balanced it is. Light peels, floral notes, and an elegant, slow, spicy warmth are a perfect foil for the other two ingredients. Aristocratic.
5*	**Martini:** Lightly vinous when wet, so dry it takes a little while to discern the gentle, relaxed pinging of botanicals across the tongue. A slow sipper.

BOTANICALS

Juniper • Orris root • Coriander seeds • Angelica root • Bitter orange peel • Lemon peel • Vanilla pod • Liquorice root • Cardamom

DUTCH COURAGE DRY GIN

44.5% ABV Netherlands

Fred van Zuidam built his distillery in the southern Dutch municipality of Baarle-Nassau in 1974. It is now run by his son Patrick, who pretty much follows the classic "can do everything" Dutch distilling template, making a range of spirits: genever, whisky, rye, liqueurs, and dry gin (*see* pp.150, 159, 174–6, and 179). This "English-style" dry gin is ultra clean on the nose with an immediate hit of citrus, backed with pine-accented juniper. In time there is a hint of coriander, adding a peppery note. The palate is bracingly citric – almost like kumquat – to start, but as soon as it begins to move, you can see how rich and almost fruity the spirit is. This interplay between silkiness, aromatics, and dryness continues along the tongue. Cardamom begins to come through on the finish with a final burst of juniper. Complex.

FLAVOUR CAMP Citric/Juniper

4	**G&T:** Although the tonic initially seems to have the upper hand here, the gin comes across well on the palate. Bone dry and refreshing.
4	**With Sicilian Lemonade:** The dryness of the gin works in this context, giving the mixer something to play with, while the lemon adds top notes. The finish maybe lacks a little in terms of length.
4.5	**Negroni:** N2 The peels are the driving force here and this ratio gives them full expression, adding marmalade and cherry. Long and mellow in the centre.
5	**Martini:** Dry, but retaining a good level of sweetness at 4:1. To see the full complexity, go drier, as the citrus flies off and reveals the hidden depth. It becomes a pretty serious drink.

BOTANICALS

Juniper • plus 28 more

FILLIERS DRY GIN 28

43.7% ABV Belgium

Made by the Belgian jenever specialist (*see* pp.170 and 177), this was created in 1928, uses 29 botanicals, and was the firm's first dry gin. The number of ingredients is often used as a selling point in gin, but can end up being no more than a marketing gimmick. Here, however, you do get the sensation of genuine botanical complexity at work. The juniper offers a sagacious and heathery start and then it's like walking into a spice market with a haunting top note that takes things into a floral/fruity realm. Water makes it slightly drier, with more orris. The palate is explosively complex. It's spicy, but the peels act as a counterfoil before the juniper returns. Just when you think it will finally dry, a sweet note emerges, kicking off another round of mini eruptions. This is 3-D gin.

FLAVOUR CAMP Juniper/Spicy

5*	**G&T:** Sometimes the bubbles have an important role to play. Here they help lift the botanicals and burst them in your nose. The aromatics and the quinine lock together in harmony. A rich G&T for after a long day.
3	**With Sicilian Lemonade:** The nose becomes more peppery but works nicely against the mixer. A little like a Gin Fizz, but the gin is slightly overwhelmed.
4	**Negroni:** N2 You need to capture the gin's complexity and even at this ratio it struggles a little. Solid and dependable.
5*	**Martini:** At 4:1, there is this slow elegance coming through, with a relaxed release of the gin's complexity. When drier, things become slightly leaner and more direct but without losing the complexity. Compelling.

BOTANICALS

Juniper • Coriander seeds • Cubeb berries • Ginger • Clove • Cardamom • Grains of paradise • Nutmeg • Cinnamon • Lemon peel • Orange peel • Liquorice root • Star anise • Cassia bark • Rosemary • Orris root • Yarrow • Lavender blossom • Blessed thistle • Hops • Gentian root • Angelica root • Carob

FLEMISH GIN 20-3

46% ABV Belgium

This was brought to my attention by Geoffrey Kelly, who himself had discovered it when on holiday. It transpires that the De Moor distillery in Aalst has been in production since 1910 and uses 23 botanicals in its dry gin. Distillation is unusual, with five separate cuts being taken during the pass, which are then blended together. Juniper is leading the way here – as you should expect in Flanders – but the vast array of other ingredients come together to create complexity. The spirit is rich and quite deep, making this almost a halfway house between jenever and dry gin. The roots have a velvety air to them, while in time there is fruitiness and spicy warm aromatics, a touch of gentian, pine, anise, sweet peels, and lavender. The palate is soft to start and then becomes more spicy, with cardamom playing a major role. This is a real discovery – thanks Geoffrey!

FLAVOUR CAMP Juniper

4	**G&T:** Has that essential juniper dip in the middle where it and the quinine start to work in balance. A serious drink.
2.5	**With Sicilian Lemonade:** While the citrus tries to give lift-off, there is too much weight for it to happen.
4.5	**Negroni:** N1 The juniper throws a thick imperial purple cloak over everything. A bold and courageous drink that should be drunk with a certain arrogant glint in the eye. Well balanced.
4	**Martini:** Surprisingly, the gin now becomes sweet with the spirit thickening well. Wetness adds to the complexity in this particular instance.

BOTANICALS

Juniper • Ginger • Liquorice root • Cassia bark • Cardamom • Coriander seeds • Cubeb berries • Nutmeg • Lime peel • Vine flower

G'VINE FLORAISON 40% ABV France

Created by Jean-Sébastien Robicquet (of Cîroc vodka fame), this is a gin that speaks profoundly of the region from which it derives, Cognac. And everything here says grapes – the base spirit is made from them, while vine flowers are one of the main botanicals, which are put into muslin bags and macerated (in grape spirit) before distillation. The other botanicals are grouped according to their character, macerated, and subsequently distilled. All the components are then blended. The gin is clear and bright, with a lifted note that is less blossom-like but more delicate fruity–floral. Then comes subtle juniper, lime, and ginger. It's highly expressive and fresh. On the palate it's quite dry with a retronasal lift of citrus and flowers, while the roots and juniper stick to the tongue. On the finish it all coheres with some cassia. Water lengthens things, the aromatics becoming slightly more flighty.

FLAVOUR CAMP Floral

5	**G&T:** Fresh floral with a real lift from the vine flower that has come fully to life. Good acidity as well, which helps in retaining freshness. The palate is full.
3.5	**With Sicilian Lemonade:** Fragrant and clean, the lime and the lemon working in tandem. All very up with a sweet mid-palate, but a little lacking in gin definition.
5	**Negroni:** N2 (made with La Quintinye Rouge) Huge cherry notes, rich, but with a luscious top note. Gentle and decadent.
4.5	**Martini:** (made with La Quintinye Extra Dry) They say it's not made for Martinis, but if you want your drink to be light and fresh, then take it out to 5:1 and sip on the terrace.

BOTANICALS

Juniper • Ginger • Liquorice root • Cassia bark • Cardamom • Coriander seeds • Cubeb berries • Nutmeg • Lime peel • Vine flower

G'VINE NOUAISON 43.9% ABV France

The second of the pair of vine flower, wine-based gins from the Cognac region (*see* opposite), this uses the small berries that emerge after flowering. At a higher strength it's been geared more towards cocktails. It's drier on the nose with a little more juniper, light coriander, and cinnamon, but has retained the fresh lime note and sweet spiciness. The palate continues this with more upfront cassia, liquorice, and cardamom yet still retains the retronasal impact of delicate floral elements. Crisper than Floraison, the finish has a similar graceful farewell, with touches of drier spices coming through on the back palate.

FLAVOUR CAMP Juniper/Spicy	
3.5	**G&T:** Rooty and dry, quite a serious G&T that suggests it's a harder drink for moments of despair. The tonic actually adds an element of sweetness to the middle.
3	**With Sicilian Lemonade:** The depth helps here to contrast the bitter lemon edges. Crisp and clean as the nose suggests, but the mixer is dominating.
5*	**Negroni:** N2 (made with La Quintinye Rouge) Big, quite dry, and rooty with serious juniper, orris, and cardamom squaring up to the cacao and black cherry of the vermouth. Excellent and muscular.
5	**Martini:** (made with La Quintinye Extra Dry) At 4:1, it works nicely, adding a juiciness to the centre, but is more impressive at 5:1 where the gin comes through more cleanly, showing its floral herbal qualities.

BOTANICALS

Juniper • Coriander seeds • Lemon peel • Black pepper • Cassia bark • Vanilla pod • Lingonberries • Meadowsweet

HERNÖ GIN 40.5% ABV Sweden

One of a new wave of gins from the fast-growing craft distilling community in the Nordics, this comes from the Hernö distillery, founded by Jon Hillgren in 2011. It may read like a classic LDG, but the effect is very different. There is an immediate mossy, herbal introduction with a very intense lemon note (almost lemon thyme/verbena) before you get pine shoot, juniper twigs, and berries. The palate manages to be both fresh and dry at the same time. There is balanced weight, a hint of coriander, and a jag of acidity, then a honeyed warmth spreads out before the juniper comes back. You can imagine having this ice cold as a shot with reindeer meat.

FLAVOUR CAMP Juniper	
X	**G&T:** In short, the gin is way too much for this.
3	**With Sicilian Lemonade:** It works much better here, as there is a bittersweet, acidic exoticism. Best at quite high dilution.
X	**Negroni:** N2 Nothing quite matches this intensity.
4.5	**Martini:** Keep it naked and you can see how this gin is very dexterously put together. I'd recommend you have some food on the side as well. Excellent.

BOTANICALS

Undeclared but chosen from a selection of 9 classic and 13 from the Cape fynbos flora

INVERROCHE CLASSIC

43% ABV South Africa

Situated in the Western Cape near Stilbaai (Still Bay), the Inverroche Distillery uses a wood-fired still with a top that looks like a mushroom. Vapour distillation is used, with the botanicals being held in a basket in the neck. A distinctive feature is the distillery's use of a mix of classic botanicals and "fynbos" – the remarkable shrubland vegetation that grows around it.

The nose is aromatic with some sharp citric notes to start things off, then becoming quite herbal and perfumed. Because of the use of fynbos, the aromas are often unfamiliar and very exciting – exotic, rooty, intense, and wild – and once opened up they show a little juniper, plus a hint of acetone. The palate is controlled at the start, with those herbal accents immediately coming over with flowers. It then softens in the centre, but turns peppery on the end.

FLAVOUR CAMP Floral/Herbal

4	**G&T:** The aroma is slightly simplified after such an exotic experience when neat. Clean and dry, it remains exotic.
4.5	**With Sicilian Lemonade:** Very intense and upfront, this is a better mix, as the herbal aspects come through well while the citrus balances.
3.5	**Negroni:** N4 The fynbos aroma is quite prominent, as you want it to be. The orange in the Campari acts as a flavour bridge, while also adding some zing to the palate.
4	**Martini:** Highly exotic and best at a 5:1 ratio, since any wetter and you get too many aromas being triggered. Crisp, clean, and fascinating.

BOTANICALS

Undeclared but include: Juniper • Coriander seeds • Orange peel

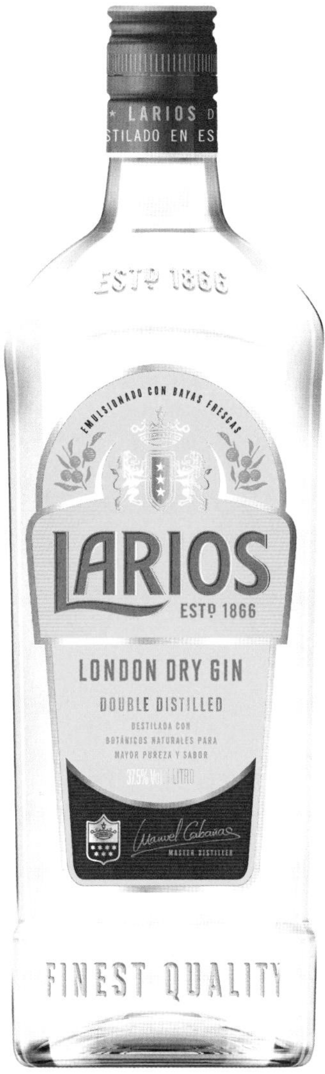

LARIOS 37.5% ABV Spain

This is Spain's biggest-selling gin, and given the volume of the spirit that the county consumes, that's a lot of bottles. The aroma is light, clean, and citric with plenty of coriander and what seems to be grapefruit peel behind. In time, there is some peppery spice, violet, and sage that then drifts off as orange peel comes out. The palate is clean and light, which is probably down to the strength, but it's a clean distillate with light dusty notes. It does, however, seem to head for an unscheduled siesta on the finish, leaving the roots slightly exposed.

FLAVOUR CAMP Citric

2.5	**G&T:** Fresh and very lemony to start with, but even at 2:1 the tonic has the bigger say. The lack of weight is the issue here.
3.5	**With Sicilian Lemonade:** Gin and Fanta Limón was one reason I chose Sicilian Lemonade, so this works. Clean, crisp, and identifiable, the limón thing offers encouragement. It's a good drink, even if not wholly a Larios drink.
3.5	**Negroni:** N2 Stuck in some deserted Spanish bar in desperate need of a Negroni? You scan and see they only have Larios. Do you change your order? No, you do not. This performs well. Not the greatest, but well short of being the poorest.
3.5	**Martini:** Needs to be longer, as the vermouth dominates at 4:1. All pleasant and clean, but making a Martini with a 37.5% gin is a big ask.

BOTANICALS

Juniper • Nutmeg • Angelica root • Coriander seeds • Lemon peel • Orange peel • Tangerine peel • Mandarin peel • Clementine peel • Grapefruit peel • Lime peel • Orange blossom

LARIOS 12 40% ABV Spain

This premium variant of Larios (*see* opposite) was made to tap into the remarkable surge of interest in top-end gins in Spain. It uses a dozen botanicals, with orange blossom being added to the still before the fourth, and final, pass. In takes the standard Larios character and turns it up to 11. The higher strength has also helped in retaining the more volatile top notes. The nose suggests that an orchard's worth of peel and blossom must have been used. It's pleasingly bittersweet, zesty, and crisp with subtle pine behind. In time, the delicacy of the blossom shows itself. The palate is elegant, if a little light. It's a bit like biting into fresh citrus fruits.

FLAVOUR CAMP Citric

3	**G&T:** Initially, it picks up a lot of lime and grapefruit. All very cool and ultra fresh with good depth. The only issue is one of persistence.
3.5	**With Sicilian Lemonade:** Here, everything is ramped up to dazzling levels. It's the slight lack of length that knocks it back.
3.5	**Negroni:** N2 All of that bouncy, energetic citrus is calmed slightly by the vermouth, which isn't necessarily a bad thing. A little herbal and light on the palate, but it's fresh and clean.
3.5	**Martini:** Up and fresh, so no need for a twist. A little light, but here the blossom, er, blossoms and acts as an interesting counterpoint to the vermouth.

BOTANICALS

Arbequina olive • Rosemary • Basil • Thyme • Juniper • Coriander seeds • Cardamom • Citrus peels

GIN MARE 42.7% ABV Spain

One of the more unusual of the New Gins, Mare is made in the Catalonian town of Vilanova i la Geltrú in a chapel that was incorporated into the site of a distillery. It's owned by the Giró family, which is behind the mass-market GIN MG brand. Mare is, however, a significant step away from MG's clean orthodoxy, since Marc and Manuel Giró wanted it to be an aromatic distillation of their particular environment – a true Mediterranean gin. The botanicals are distilled either separately or in combination to give six distillates that are then blended. Rather than juniper, the nose offers up olive, basil, thyme, and a touch of marmalade. In due course, you get aniseed and a hint of pepper and then rosemary. Only with water do the purple berries declare their presence. The palate seems slightly sweetened but begins to dry in the middle, which is where the fresh herbs come out. It's balanced, really well distilled... but is it gin? In today's world, yes, it is.

FLAVOUR CAMP Floral/Herbal

4	**G&T:** Clean and with good retention of character. The tonic works well in tandem with the herbs.
4.5	**With Sicilian Lemonade:** Fragrant and where the slightly more forgiving mixer works a little better. Light, but with no loss of character.
3.5	**Negroni:** N4 Olives are the main issue here. Great in other drinks, but not when put up with vermouth. Becomes a little like red pesto.
4.5	**Martini:** Who needs to add an olive to their Martini if you have Mare? Lengthy, sightly oily, and aromatically intense.

BOTANICALS

Some say only juniper is used

MASCARÓ GIN 9 40% ABV Spain

Produced by the Mascaró family in Vilafranca de Penedès in a London Dry style, this signifies a move away from the Spanish herbs and citrus axis. The nose is well balanced and slightly waxy, with some penetrating lemony notes and juniper to the fore. There is pine sap and there are pine needles, a little touch of cough sweets, and, in time, a slight chalkiness. The palate is very pure and clean, with a rich and slightly resinous mid-palate. Altogether it has good balance.

FLAVOUR CAMP Juniper

3	**G&T:** Quite mild and slightly earthy, with a light mid-palate and some lift. Pleasant.
4	**With Sicilian Lemonade:** Better and clean, allowing more of the gin to come through, especially its sweeter aspects. Again, a lovely balance is struck.
4	**Negroni:** N2The juniper might suggest having this as a classic 1:1:1 ratio, but there is a delicacy about the gin, so I've scaled the vermouth and Campari back. The gin adds a light drying element to the mix. It's a very coolly poised gin, so be careful.
4	**Martini:** Good at 4:1 and 5:1, with the latter showing the depth of the spirit. The vermouth is only there to offer a helping hand. It has some class.

BOTANICALS

Juniper • Angelica root • Coriander seeds • Orris root • Liquorice root • Nutmeg • Cubeb berries • Clove • Cardamom • Cassia bark • Cinnamon • Grains of paradise • Almond • Ginger • Sage • Lavender • Acacia flowers • Hibiscus • Bee balm • Honeysuckle • Jasmine • Chamomile • Bramble leaves • Lingonberries • Spruce shoots • Pepper (six types) • Acacia • Calamus root • Lemon verbena • Lemon balm • Lemon grass • Pomelo • Bitter orange peel • Kaffir lime leaves • Blackberries • Cranberries • Dog rose • Elderflower • Hawthorn berries • Rosehips • Sloes • plus Purple shamrock in this bottle

MONKEY 47 SCHWARZWALD DRY GIN 47% ABV Germany

Wing Commander "Monty" Collins arrived in the Black Forest in 1951, opening a guest house called Zum Wilden Affen, "The Wild Monkey". He started to distil gin using local botanicals, such as juniper, lingonberries, and spruce shoots. After his death, the legend of his gin lived on, but it was thought that there was no record of his recipe. However, at the turn of the century, an old bottle of "Max the Monkey" gin was found along with a letter describing the plant ingredients used. Alexander Stein worked with fruit distiller Christoph Keller to revive it. A complex 47-botanical gin, this is highly aromatic with a menthol/camphor lead, then fruits followed by high-toned perfume and zest. The palate alternates between sweet, spicy, acidic, and savoury. A light peppery edge is balanced by intense citrus and herbal notes, with the finish showing dark berries. A slow sipper with ice.

FLAVOUR CAMP Floral/Herbal

X **G&T:** Not applicable.

X **With Sicilian Lemonade:** Not applicable.

X **Negroni:** Not applicable.

5* **Martini:** Best naked or ultra dry with just a whisper of vermouth. Why add more flavour?

BOTANICALS

Including: Juniper • Citrus peels • Orris root • Liquorice root • White peach • Turkish rose • Raspberry

NOLET'S SILVER DRY GIN

47.6% ABV Netherlands

The Nolet family has been distilling in Schiedam, the capital of Dutch genever, since 1691. Ironically, most of the world knows them best for their Ketel One vodka, but their gin roots run deep. The family's newest gin is, however, some considerable distance away from the type of spirit that Johannes Nolet would have made 10 generations back. Silver is uncompromisingly a New Gin. The use of fruit and flower essences – made for Nolet's by a French perfume house – makes this a fruit bomb of a gin with raspberry, chews, candyfloss, Starburst sweets, and no discernible juniper. It struck me as being a little like a teenage girl's perfume and my own teenage daughter agreed: Lush Snow Fairy to be precise. There is just a hint of *parfait amour*. The palate is sweet and thick with those perfumes flying over the top, and a hint of camphor at the end. Maybe I'm not the target market.

FLAVOUR CAMP Floral/Fragrant

2.5 **G&T:** Not particularly enhanced by the tonic, it is sweet and candyfloss-like. A drink for the fairground?

3.5 **With Sicilian Lemonade:** This is bonkers. The mixer at least gives the gin something to work against – or at least bind itself to – and while sweet, it kinda works.

3.5 **Negroni:** N4 The sheer "pinkness" of the gin is (forcibly) restrained here and makes quite a pleasant drink – if you like Turkish Delight.

3 **Martini:** It works initially, and again if a sweeter, more confected drink is your bag, then this is the gin for you.

BOTANICALS

Juniper • Coriander seeds • Angelica root • Cinnamon • Ginger • Lemon peel • Bitter orange peel • Curaçao orange • Chamomile • Lavender • Elderflower

TELSER LIECHTENSTEIN DRY GIN 47% ABV Liechtenstein

The Telser family has been producing fruit spirits in Liechtenstein since 1880 and runs the only commercial distillery in the tiny principality. Although it declares itself to be a London Dry and the botanicals are not that unusual, distiller Marcel Telser clearly has some Alpine tricks up his sleeve, though he won't say what they are. It is ultra-clean and fresh, with a herbaceous opening backed with light juniper. As it warms, it becomes more floral with green notes, some pollen, and a grassiness. In other words, it's alpine. The palate shows how highly perfumed it is, with masses of Parma violet and good weight from the spirit, before juniper reveals itself alongside lavender.

FLAVOUR CAMP Floral/Herbal	
3.5	**G&T:** Is this too perfumed? Some may think so, in which case try lengthening it, where the combination works well.
3.5	**With Sicilian Lemonade:** The acidity of the mixer helps to balance all the elements here and the perfume is controlled. Again, best when taken long.
4	**Negroni:** N2 The alpine intensity continues and it definitely works better with Aperol rather than Campari. The palate is clean and penetrating, with the gin singing out fully.
4	**Martini:** Pretty and lifted. Again, there is the blast of an alpine meadow. Best at 5:1, otherwise you could suffer from herbal overload.

BOTANICALS

Juniper • Lemon peel

VAN WEES THREE-CORNER DRY GIN 42% ABV Netherlands

The firm of A. van Wees has been working in genever (and gin) since 1782 and is the last distillery still operational in Amsterdam. As well as a range of 17 genevers, they also make dry gins, such as this, which, in their words, "respects the English influence". Although it's more aromatically forward rather than distillate-driven, only two botanicals, juniper and lemon peel, are used. It has a very clean, penetrating nose with plenty of fresh lemon and pine, and provides a clear demonstration of how naturally these two aromas bind together. It says it's dry, and it is. The palate is smooth, with good complexity on the mid-palate. Just by using two botanicals, you can see how juniper plays at the top, in the middle, and in the base of a gin. This is really good.

FLAVOUR CAMP Juniper

3.5	**G&T:** A classic LDG attack with juniper and an earthy note from the quinine. Maybe a little short, but fair.
4	**With Sicilian Lemonade:** Well mixed and clean, with the citrus a natural partner and the sweeter elements in the mixer adding a little breadth to the palate. I'd be more than happy with this in front of me.
4	**Negroni:** N1 The classic ratio works well here, with that maraschino, rooty dark depth, sage, and pine, then bittersweet elements beginning to be let loose. Lovely balance.
4	**Martini:** Quite oily and rich, giving the tongue something to work with and becoming more perfumed as it warms in the mouth. Works equally well at 5:1.

BOTANICALS

Not fully declared but include: Juniper • Orris root • Cinnamon • Orange peel • Rose petals

VICTORIA GIN 45% ABV Canada

Victoria Spirits, based just outside, er, Victoria, on Vancouver Island, started to produce gin in 2008, making it one of the earliest of Canada's craft distillers. It claims to be the first to produce gin, and uses a mix of classic and locally sourced botanicals, such as rose petals. This has an oily start with a little turmeric edge suggesting that a very creamy base spirit is being used. There is a little cassia, some coriander, and a marshmallow-like background note. With water there are a few more herbal/piney green elements with fresh juniper berries and fennel seeds. The palate is as thick and buttery as the nose suggests, but the botanicals are bold enough to make themselves heard. It's almost the same weight as a genever and could (maybe should) be treated the same way. A gingery thrust makes the finish quite energetic. Water renders things a little too soft, so I would leave the drinks hard.

FLAVOUR CAMP Spicy

3.5	**G&T:** Retains a slightly herbal element reminiscent of woodruff and sweet cicely. The higher dilution is better here to achieve good balance.
4	**With Sicilian Lemonade:** A fair accord between the two elements. The lemon adds length. This would also work well as a Fizz.
3.5	**Negroni:** N2 The fat spirit comes through. The vermouth helps in distributing the flavours nicely, adding a softness.
3.5	**Martini:** Clean with more violet notes initially. That heavy creamy element helps here at low temperatures, adding weight before cinnamon comes through. Has character. Also try it as a Martinez.

BOTANICALS

Undeclared but 12 including: Juniper • Coriander seeds • Lemon myrtle • Lime peel • Wattle seeds

THE WEST WINDS GIN THE SABRE 40% ABV Australia

In 2009, James Clarke and Paul White decided to put the still that the latter had imported to good use. With Jeremy Spencer and Jason Chan also in tow, they set up the Tailor Made Spirits Company in Margaret River, Western Australia, of which The West Winds was the first release. Their brace of gins (the other being The Cutlass) utilize classic LDG botanicals, as well as a judicious addition of those native to the region. In The Sabre, it is the distinctive penetrating note of lemon myrtle that comes across first, followed by lime and grapefruit-like citrus – all very intense with some sagebrush-like juniper in the background. As it opens, there is menthol; the palate is aromatic and light, with floral hints and a cooling quality. This is a long, aromatic New Gin with just enough juniper at the end to slow it down, and overall an excellent balance. A name to watch.

FLAVOUR CAMP Citric

4	**G&T:** Balanced and still very up, with good persistence. Equally good if taken longer, as it retains character.
5	**With Sicilian Lemonade:** An intriguing mix this, as you have all the aromas complementing each other rather than overloading things. Very refreshing and recommended.
4	**Negroni:** N2 Clean with a fresh bittersweet start. Immediately a classy drink with good peels, juniper, and a rich weight to the mid-palate. A summery Negroni, but it's always summer in Margaret River.
4.5	**Martini:** Too wet at 4:1, but when drier the full character of the gin comes across, bringing out herbal eucalypt. Clean and dry with plenty character.

BOTANICALS

Undeclared

XORIGUER 38% ABV Spain

Gin was first made on the Balearic Island of Menorca in the eighteenth century when it was held by the British (between 1713–56, 1763–83, and 1798–1802). Strategically important, it was home to a large garrison of thirsty troops and sailors who began demanding gin. Juniper was imported, wine was distilled, and Mahon gin was born. Xoriguer appeared as a brand in the 1920s. The botanical recipe is a secret, but certainly involves juniper and local herbs, and it's given a short period in vats to mellow. The nose opens with a blast of wild fennel pollen, then a dry bitter edge that hints at wormwood. Next is sweet cicely, then comes rosemary, mint, and a celery-like angelica. Juniper is understated. The spirit is almost meaty and on the palate you pick up bay, herbs, and by now assertive coriander along with what seems to be cumin, aniseed, and lavender. There is no gin quite like it.

FLAVOUR CAMP Floral/Herbal	
4	**G&T:** In character; the tonic does help to slightly curb the lavender on the palate, but also brings out sage notes. Perfumed, different, and with decent persistence.
2	**With Sicilian Lemonade:** The meaty element in the spirit is brought out here, and the flavours are now too herbal.
3	**Negroni:** N2 It has to be at this ratio to put a brake on the aromatics of the gin, but no matter what you do you will always end up in the dusty hills of Menorca.
4	**Martini:** Like drinking a herb garden. Perfumed and quite oily, but with real style.

AMERICAN

It all started with a reaction against industrial beer and the subsequent emergence of America's mighty and continually evolving craft-brewing movement. In time, many of these brewers decided to branch out into distilling, but with the same founding principles: small-scale, local, premium. From the start, gin was part of their plan. They joined some existing specialist distillers, then had their numbers boosted by bartenders, historians, and writers; the curious wanting to make something that was new and different.

Some looked to distillation techniques, others to the past to create a "what if" scenario of American gin had Prohibition never happened. They foraged and macerated, they read and wrote manifestos, they sprang up in urban areas and farmland, in forests and one-horse towns. Some rejected juniper, others held it close; some used neutral spirit, others a lower-strength base.

America "made" gin, but America, ironically, had never really made gin. That situation has now changed. This is a new, exciting frontier for gin and one that is continually evolving.

BOTANICALS

Lavender • Sarsaparilla • Coriander seeds • Cardamom • Juniper • Aniseed • Sweet orange peel

AVIATION 42% ABV

Aviation came into being thanks to a meeting of minds and talents: the distilling team at Portland, Oregon's House Spirits Distillery and bartender Ryan Magarian. It was launched in 2006 as one of the new "New Western" gins, in which the makers felt that juniper need not play such a forward role. Like many New Gin distillers, Aviation not only dialled down the juniper to create "a botanical democracy" but added some new aromatics, in their case sarsaparilla. Broad and slightly fleshy on the nose with a background powderiness, initially it's quite high-toned with cardamom, a little lavender, and a touch of mintiness, lime, and coriander. The palate has an intriguing mix of the bittersweet, a floral lift to start that deepens into spice, and a hint of pine on the very end. This gin is at the forefront of the New Western brigade.

FLAVOUR CAMP Spicy

4	**G&T:** At the start quite overwhelming and floral with a big hint of aniseed and a bittersweet edge, which could be that sarsaparilla. More spices - cardamom in particular. It's not your average G&T, but then it doesn't want to be.
2.5	**With Sicilian Lemonade:** The mixer adds some citrus, but the overall effect is a little flat.
3.5	**Negroni:** N3 Clean with plenty of the sarsaparilla and cardamom to the fore. Sets up quite a pungent punch with the vermouth. Intense is the word.
3.5	**Martini:** The dryness of the gin is brought out here, so needs to be balanced by the vermouth, which means that 4:1 is ideal. Becomes quite a spicy drink.

BOTANICALS

Juniper • Coriander seeds • Bitter orange peel • Grains of paradise • Angelica root • Cassia bark • Orris root • Cardamom • Tasmanian pepperberries

BIG GIN 47% ABV

Although Seattle gin specialist Captive Spirits is a relative newcomer to the scene – it was set up by Ben and Holly Capdevielle in 2011 – it doesn't ride with the New Western gang (*see* opposite). Anyone weaned on classic juniper-forward dry gins will recognize this as a kindred spirit. Citrus ignites the procession of aromas, closely followed by very purple juniper, with that bright berry note that comes through in some of the American New Gins, which in turn could be down to supporting botanicals. The palate shows it to be gentle and soft in texture (the botanicals rest on a corn base spirit), with a peppery note from coriander and (presumably) pepperberry. It remains spicy on the finish, and is overall very well balanced and controlled. Even the crustiest of traditionalists will be impressed by this.

FLAVOUR CAMP Juniper

4.5	**G&T:** Works nicely, with pretty classic juniper/roots giving crunch to the palate, citrus and pepper topping and tailing. Becomes a little sweeter and lasts well. It does need a citrus wedge though.
3.5	**With Sicilian Lemonade:** As with tonic, the sweetness at this gin's heart comes through, although I'm not sure that the bitterness of the lemon is the ideal partner.
3.5	**Negroni:** N1 Big and punchy, with that peppery element adding some tingle to the tongue. Maybe a little too sweet for classicists, but it works.
4	**Martini:** 4:1 is simply too wet – the juniper is too strong a component here – but bring it out to 5:1 and it works, as long as you like classically Dry Martinis with a juniper/rooty flow. Peppery tail-off. Good.

BOTANICALS

Juniper • Orris root • Coriander seeds • Angelica root • Cardamom • Lemon peel • Orange peel

COLD RIVER 47% ABV

Founded in Freeport, Maine, in 2005 by Chris Dowe, Cold River's claim to fame is that its spirits (it makes gin and vodka) are based on potato; Maine potatoes, to be precise, grown by partner Donnie Thibodeau at Green Thumb Farms. The gin, which was launched in 2010, has a base of triple-distilled pot-still potato spirit. The start has quite a penetrating piney juniper (this is very much in lime with classic dry gins rather than the New Western approach – *see* p.138) with light lemony coriander and angelica in its sweet green leafy expressiveness. Water brings out light citrus, more cardamom, and a general floral note. The nature of potato spirit plays its part as well, particularly on the palate where its creaminess comes through. The juniper is retained, but the aromas become increasingly lifted, with a long, ripe finish.

FLAVOUR CAMP Juniper/Floral

3.5 **G&T:** Allows the tonic to bring the botanicals forward, juniper and cardamom especially. Quite creamy still, which makes this a pretty weighty drink that some might want to lengthen.

3.5 **With Sicilian Lemonade:** Now it's the turn of the roots to come through. The palate remains rich, but the citrus picks up freshness.

3.5 **Negroni:** N1 The richness of the spirit means that it ends up slightly sweeter, so scale back the vermouth in particular. More floral characters begin to emerge. Decent balance.

3.5 **Martini:** 4:1 makes it really big boned, so it's worthwhile upping the gin. Floral again, with more cardamom. Clean but certainly rich.

BOTANICALS

Juniper • Coriander seeds • Fennel seeds

DEATH'S DOOR 47% ABV

In 2005, The Death's Door Distillery opened on Washington Island (which lies between Green Bay and Lake Michigan) with the laudable aim of being as local as possible. The base is a locally grown wheat/barley malt-based spirit, while the botanicals are a very simple mix of juniper (from the island) and Michigan-grown coriander and fennel. The intense lemony/fruity note that comes out early on makes you wonder if Michigan coriander is different, while the piney juniper has a resinous berry brightness. On the palate, the juniper becomes more lavender-like, then there is an explosive spicy–fruity coriander note in the centre, before aniseed starts to build, along with a light mineral note. The base spirit has a generous feel, unusual in dry gins but might ring bells with those who have tried genever.

FLAVOUR CAMP Juniper

3	**G&T:** More aniseed with the tonic now, and it needs fresh citrus to compensate for the lack of peels. Dry, persistent, but a little lacking on the back palate.
3.5	**With Sicilian Lemonade:** Lemon seems to dominate, but the palate shows how well it balances. Clean and quite long.
4	**Negroni:** N1 This works at the classic ratio, as you need the Campari to weigh in quite strongly. Don't worry; the gin is rich enough to cope, while fennel and vermouth have a natural affinity.
4	**Martini:** The texture of the spirit reveals itself. A gentle release with more aniseed coming out. Stick to 4:1 to allow more herbal element to add complexity. Try La Quintinye Extra Dry or Vya Extra Dry.

BOTANICALS

Juniper • Dried hibiscus • Elderberry • Orange peel • Lemon peel • Grapefruit peel • Cinnamon

DOROTHY PARKER 44% ABV

This is made in Brooklyn by the New York Distilling Company (Allen Katz and Tom Potter - *see also* p.181) and named after the legendary writer, wit, and - more significantly in this instance - gin drinker. It's not as acerbic as Dorothy, opening with a tightly focused citric burst followed by fruit and flowers, with terpene juniper notes in the background adding structure and depth; very much a modernist take on some very old principles. The palate shows more of the heavy floral richness, which now turns the juniper more lavender-like. All of this is balanced by zesty citrus - grapefruit is the most prominent - coriander, and finally some cassia. In its neat state, so much is vying for attention that the addition of water is a relief, when every element ceases trying to outdo the others at the table and the true balance is revealed. It manages to have a dry gin's austerity with a heavy floral depth.

FLAVOUR CAMP Floral

4	**G&T:** Everything is well integrated and balanced. Very fresh, zingy, and citric. Best taken at 1:2.
3	**With Sicilian Lemonade:** I'd have thought that all the peels would have made this a no-brainer, but the overall effect is a bit clumsy.
4.5	**Negroni:** N2 More of the grapefruit and flowers here, which meld with Campari, but the elderberry and juniper are working hard behind the scenes building alliances with the vermouth. Becomes very rich.
4	**Martini:** Lots of fruit peels and flowers, and while there is an initial standoff between juniper and vermouth, they end up in harmony. It louches (turns opaque) at low temperatures.

BOTANICALS

Juniper • Coriander seeds • Chamomile • Elderflower • Citrus peels • Thai blue ginger • Cinnamon • Orris root • Elderberry

GREENHOOK GINSMITHS AMERICAN DRY 47% ABV

In recent years, Brooklyn has become a centre for artisan distillers. The DeAngelo brothers, Steven and Philip, started their dedicated gin production in 2012. Production – off a wheat-based spirit – is in a copper pot still that is run under vacuum, giving a lower boiling point, which, the theory goes, increases the intensity of the botanicals without any vegetal or stewed aromas coming over. It does share an intense penetrating opening with other American New Gins. Here, it's a kumquat-like citric element with some green fruit and florals. It then becomes slightly more orthodox as juniper and coriander come out (fear not, it's still gin). Equally fresh on the palate, it shows more chamomile, with juniper setting up shop in the middle of the tongue over a dusty, spiced background.

FLAVOUR CAMP Citric	
4	**G&T:** The florals come through more clearly here (even more so with Fever-Tree Elderflower Tonic); a good level of complexity. Crisp and dry, if just a tad bitter.
4.5	**With Sicilian Lemonade:** The citric opening returns. Zesty and quite long, with a soft centre and low spice.
4	**Negroni:** N2 More juniper emerges now and this mix allows you to experience the gin at its best. Good balance and integration.
3.5	**Martini:** Clean and very pure, but needs the vermouth to put some flesh on its bones.

BOTANICALS

Undeclared but officially "more than a dozen" – there is certainly juniper!

JUNÍPERO 49.3% ABV

Fritz Maytag, the founder of San Francisco's Anchor Distilling, liked to ask those awkward questions that challenge orthodoxies. What would a 100 per cent rye whiskey be like? How would a juniper-heavy gin taste? His answers were liquid re-creations from America's rich distilling heritage. The arrival of Junípero in 1996 didn't just re-create a taste of the past but demonstrated that premium artisan spirits could be made in the USA. It started an American New Gin revolution.

Junípero's nose is all terpene-rich juniper with some supporting lemony coriander. I think it's become less extreme than it was in the nineties (or maybe the world has simply caught up), as there is some citrus on top as well as a muscular violet note. The palate is soft, rich, and unapologetically pungent. Not only symbolically important, this tastes great.

FLAVOUR CAMP Juniper

5	**G&T:** I thought it might be too much for the mixer, but the tonic takes it on *mano a mano* and a sweet fatness comes through. The botanical depth is open with more cinnamon. Balanced. It does need citrus, but works very well.
3	**With Sicilian Lemonade:** Slightly bitter, which is no bad thing if there is enough sweetness, but I'm not sure quite enough is present.
5	**Negroni:** N1 Muted nose and a dry start, then huge cherry, cacao, and pine come through. Rich, deep, bitter, and deadly serious.
5	**Martini:** At 4:1, it's fresh, vinous, clean, botanicals-effusive, and brilliantly drying on the tongue. Even here it might be too dry for some.

LEOPOLD'S NAVY STRENGTH

57% ABV

BOTANICALS

Undeclared but include: Juniper • Coriander seeds • Cardamom • Bergamot

The Leopold brothers, Todd and Scott, began craft brewing in Michigan in 1999 and expanded into distilling two years later. Today their operations are in Denver, Colorado. For the Navy Strength they have removed the pomelo from their Small Batch gin and replaced it with the more intense bergamot. The amount of juniper has been doubled, while coriander and cardamom have both been upped. All are distilled separately. Surprisingly, this Spinal Tap approach, with those big aromatics turned up to 11, has not just made things more junipery, nor has the high strength made things too hot. Instead, there is a bouquet's worth of peachy, floral essence released with a big bergamot hit. In time, it becomes more like a perfumed juniper eau-de-vie, with notes like lemon grass and white pepper, then an estery, perfumed note, while the palate retains an almost Turkish Delight quality before a bergamot, pine, and roots finish.

FLAVOUR CAMP Floral/Citric/Juniper

3.5	**G&T:** The tonic helps to dry things down, reducing this potpourri of aromas. Good balance and cleanliness.
3.5	**With Sicilian Lemonade:** Clean and vibrant, the flowers being held in check.
3.5	**Negroni:** N4 Intense. The floral aspect and bergamot behave like hooligans with the Campari to start with, while the juniper initially sulks. Then it reaches out and manacles itself to the vermouth. A boisterous mix.
4	**Martini:** The higher alcohol helps to give this a very unctuous feel, and the vermouth (when at a 5:1 ratio) adds a pleasant green note. More juniper comes across and the bergamot is better balanced.

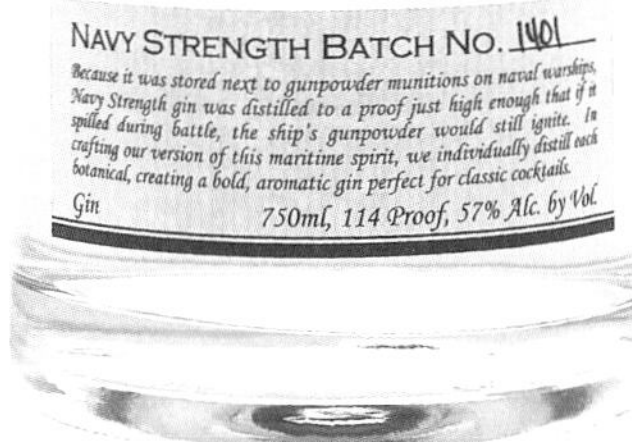

BOTANICALS

Not fully declared but officially "between 8 and 11", including: Juniper • Bergamot • Lemon peel • Cardamom • Cassia bark • Angelica root • Coriander seeds

NO. 209 46% ABV

Launched in 2005, No. 209 comes from a distillery that perches over the water on San Francisco's Pier 50. It was founded by Leslie Rudd, who owned Dean & DeLuca and is still proprietor of Rudd Oakville Estate Winery and Edge Hill Estate (which is where the original Distillery No. 209 was located). Its 7.5-metre (25-foot) tall still was modelled on those in the Glenmorangie's whisky distillery, which isn't as surprising as it seems, since Glenmo's were originally taken from Edward Taylor's gin distillery in Chelsea (*see* p.63). No. 209 opens with fresh citrus – lemon, lime, and bergamot – before some gentle juniper emerges over a discreet floral back note. The palate has a mass of citrus to start, a substantial mid-palate showing lavender, fennel, and celery, and a warm cardamom and cassia-accented finish. This is a serious and balanced gin.

FLAVOUR CAMP Spicy/Citric	
5*	**G&T:** Glorious, with a real lemon lift. One of those combinations where everything pulls together and is enhanced. A quintessential G&T. Excellent.
4.5	**With Sicilian Lemonade:** Naturally it's citric, but although the gin slides away slightly, there is weight and oiliness that fleshes out the mid-palate.
4.5	**Negroni:** N2 Quite dry and very spicy. Cardamom is the trigger here, sitting in the centre and influencing everything. There is a dried herb note, and it remains quite sweet and cherry-like with light bergamot.
5	**Martini:** The vermouth contributes a herbal backing, and its vinosity adds to the texture and brings a gentle sweetness. Highly complex and gently flowing. Equally good and more classical at 5:1.

BOTANICALS

Juniper • Angelica root • Bay laurel • Bergamot • Black peppercorns • Caraway seeds • Cardamom • Coriander leaves • Coriander seeds • Cinnamon • Citra hops • Dill seeds • Fennel seeds • Ginger • Lemon peel • Lime peel • Orris root • Seville orange peel • Star anise

ST. GEORGE BOTANIVORE

45% ABV

Jörg Rupf started making eau-de-vie at his St George Spirits distillery in 1982. Since then, the distillery has expanded to fill an aircraft hangar (where Hangar One vodka was born) and the portfolio to include single malt whiskey, absinthe, rum, and, from 2011, gin. This is its celebration of botanicals – 19 of them. The distillation involves putting three (juniper, bay laurel, and coriander leaves) in a vapour basket while the others are steeped before everything is distilled. The aroma is garrigue-like, with a huge herbal impact, then comes heady citrus with bergamot poking through before hints of pine, followed by wild greens. The palate repeats these elements but with more aniseed, and only on the end does the juniper come out of the miasma holding hands with orris and cardamom. It's focused, complex, and generous.

FLAVOUR CAMP Herbal/Spicy	
4	**G&T:** That herbaceous/leafy note returns and there is some sweetness on the centre. It's a big and complex G&T that needs a bit of lengthening.
3.5	**With Sicilian Lemonade:** Clean and good, but like some multiple botanical gins the mixer fails to find focus.
3	**Negroni:** N1 Here, that herbal note offers a link to the vermouth, while the peels (especially bergamot) go to the Campari. It's a huge and almost baffling array. I'd keep things simple, so...
4.5	**Martini:** ...use it in here. In fact, have it naked – there is no need for more herbs. Becomes more piney, spiced, aniseedy, and dry. Great.

BOTANICALS

12 in total but the only ones declared are: Sage • Douglas fir • Juniper • Roasted coriander seeds • Bay laurel

ST. GEORGE TERROIR GIN

45% ABV

Distilling eau-de-vie, which is how St. George's founder Jörg Rupf and its current owner/master distiller Lance Winters started (*see* p.147), means capturing the purest essence of the ingredient, and this concept is central to understanding the firm's Terroir gin. This is not just a distillation of botanicals but that of a place, specifically the forests and chaparral behind the distillery. There is Douglas fir, sage, juniper, and bay laurel, as well as wok-roasted coriander seeds (it's not native, but Winters says that the roasted seeds smell like the chaparral). The sage and fir are distilled separately, the juniper and bay in a vapour basket, the rest in the body of the still. The result is a hallucinatory plunge into a forest. There is pine, resin, a sage note, a velvety menthol lift, citrus, a big geranium-like laurel note, bay rum, bruised spices, juniper, and then herbal aniseed. It gets even rootier with water. On the palate there is massive retronasal impact. It's a trip.

FLAVOUR CAMP Juniper

X	**G&T:** Too massively complex.
X	**With Sicilian Lemonade:** It really doesn't work here either.
X	**Negroni:** The nose offers hope. I mean it's as OTT as you would expect, but the palate is a pile-up.
5*	**Martini:** Have it naked and start by running through a moist, old-growth forest. Immense amounts of fir, pine, and bay. End up sweating in a hogan scented with sage incense. Love it.

OTHER GINS

In our lust for the new, we can forget what has come before. Thankfully, one of the key elements of being a distiller is having a keen awareness of the past. Styles are kept alive because of a mercifully stubborn belief in their quality. Genever is one of those styles.

This is where gin came from, yet it has been ignored by drinkers in its native lands and misrepresented by the rest of the world. No longer. Genever is now, once again, a player on the world stage. It's a link to gin's past, and a bridge between gin and whisky – another facet of gin's future. Please do not pass it by. These are remarkable spirits.

Bartenders, too, have a deep appreciation of what has come before, and with gin's revival came a resurgence of interest in old-style drinks. To make them, they needed "old-style" gins, and distillers obliged. We are now, joyously, in a world where Old Tom is once again being made and being drunk, a world where cask-rested gins are being appreciated.

The same goes for fruit gins: the sultriness of sloe or damson, the sweetness of raspberry, or any other fruit you can imagine. You can buy it ready-made in bottles, but you can also make your own. All you need is access to ripe fruit, a freezer to pop it into for a day, good-quality gin, an empty bottle that you half-fill with the fruit and top up with gin, and time (I'd say 12 weeks). Oh, and some simple syrup or gomme (*see* p.188) for adjusting the sweetness after it's ready.

BOTANICALS

Juniper • Orris root • Coriander seeds • Angelica root • Sweet orange peel • Fresh whole lemons • Liquorice root • Cardamom • Vanilla pod

DUTCH COURAGE OLD TOM'S GIN 40% ABV Netherlands

It was only a matter of time before Patrick van Zuidam made an Old Tom. After all, he's done every other style of gin and genever (*see* pp.119, 159, 174–6, and 179). Released in 2013, this has also been rested in cask for a short period, adding a light lemony hue, while the oak notes are there from the off. The spices are quite dry, meaning that the nose has no real indication of sweetness. Instead, there is preserved lemon (whole lemons are used) tied into coriander, pungent spice, and a light nuttiness. Rather than taking it neat, best add a drop of water to soften the aroma and make it more expressive. Only then does the piney juniper come out. The palate, however, is clearly Old Tom with honeyed, fruit syrup notes emerging alongside mint, juniper, coriander, and Christmassy spices. The oak is balanced and lightly vanillic. Water again make things cohere and amplifies the texture. It's rich certainly, but not cloying; indeed, the finish begins to dry slightly.

4	**Gin Cocktail:** Quite malty with a good impact from the bitters, with coriander and cardamom more prominent on the palate. Punchy.
3.5	**Gin Fizz:** Again, slightly nutty to start, but the extra sweetness allows the lemon juice to come through and scales back the oak.
4	**Martinez:** It's too fat and sweet as a Martinez, but when adjusted to Turf Club proportions, it works much better, with a hint of bitterness to act as a counterweight.

BOTANICALS

Undeclared

JENSEN'S OLD TOM 43% ABV UK

There is a significant difference between Jensen's Old Tom and all the other Old Toms on the market: no sweetening is used. So how, you may ask quite reasonably, is this an Old Tom? Because Christian Jensen believes that in Old Tom's heyday sugar wasn't used – it was too expensive – and that the sweetness came from botanicals instead. The debate continues. No surprise then that this is a very different type of Old Tom. Big and quite broad, in the Jensen style, the spirit seems to have more of a say here. This is from his new Bermondsey distillery (*see* p.93), and has a slight malty/nutty touch that takes it closer to genever. Juniper is high up in the mix, with an earthy rootiness and some peppery coriander, but little in way of any citric uplift. Water adds some florals and a note similar to sesame oil. The palate seems very dry to start, with pine and sage. The sweetening is really very subtle, making this more of an off-dry gin. Water improves it in terms of spread and complexity.

X	**G&T:** Massive impact, but on the palate the tonic goes one way, the Old Tom the other.
3.5	**Gin Fizz:** You need to dose up the drink with more sugar in order to hit a decent balance here. When you do, it's quite rooty yet decent.
4	**Martinez:** The best of the trio (these Victorians knew what they were doing). The maraschino is the key here, picking up the violet edge and running with it, then linking into the cherry depth in the vermouth. Decent.

BOTANICALS

Juniper • Coriander seeds • Angelica root • Lemon peel • Orange peel • Orris root • Cardamom • Cassia bark • Liquorice root • Cinnamon • Nutmeg

HAMMER & SON OLD ENGLISH GIN 44% ABV UK

Although this doesn't declare itself to be an Old Tom, it doesn't need to. This is a re-creation of a recipe from 1783 and, at that point, gin was sweetened. The bottle itself even reflects the times before gin was bottled by producers. Distillers would supply gin to merchants who would either store it in cask or bottle it, maybe in their own branded bottles, or into whatever was around. Clearly the merchant here also did a roaring trade in Champagne. It's all very well thought through, as you might expect from Henrik Hammer (*see* p.85) The gin – made at Langley (*see* p.75) – is excellent. The sweetness isn't too overt (4 grams per litre is the dose), but well integrated into the mix, adding weight to the forward green, woody notes of angelica, oily juniper, and crisp spiciness. There is a sense of a mass of flavour being held in check. Water releases sage, heather, and more coriander, while the palate has a fizzy, lemony, vibrant nature that counters the very subtle sweetening, which liquorice also helps along. This is a balanced, serious gin.

3.5	**G&T:** Assertive, with plenty of rooty elements. The Old Tom sweetness only kicks in quite late on, balancing out the roots and quinine. Decent.
4	**Gin Fizz:** Very clean and zesty, with excellent expressiveness from the gin. Lip-smackingly clean and balanced.
5	**Martinez:** The gentle nature of the gin's sweetness means that it isn't too sugary when the vermouth is added. Instead, you pick up more bitter notes and richness. Complex, balanced, and with a savoury edge.

BOTANICALS

Juniper • Coriander seeds • Nutmeg • Cinnamon • Orange peel • Lemon peel • Angelica root • Orris root • Cassia bark • Liquorice root

HAYMAN'S OLD TOM 40% ABV UK

The launch of Hayman's Old Tom in 2007 was a sign that gin was once again being taken seriously – by bartenders at least. An interest in old drinks and a lack of Old Tom would make the decision an easy one you would think, but it was still a risk. Bartenders may want it, but would the public want to drink sweetened gin? It's one thing making a drink purely for fun, quite another to make it commercially viable. The fact that it is still around shows that the distiller was right. This gin is from an 1870s Hayman family recipe and sticks to the firm's botanical line-up but in a slightly different ratio and, obviously, with sweetening. Here you get more of the perfumed violet aspect coming out, along with some orange, liquorice, and a little marzipan. The sweetness seems to give everything a gentle push along, and there is eucalyptus, peels, and gingerbread when water is added. The palate is mellow, still allowing acidity from the citrus (orange especially) to come through. It thickens rather than sweetens. You lose the crisp definition of LDG, but without sacrificing any levels of complexity. Job done.

3.5	**G&T:** Works well on the nose, bringing out more top notes. The sweetness slightly skews things on the palate though and it becomes a little flat.
4	**Gin Fizz:** Zesty and lively, with the sweetness of the gin countering the attack of the lemon. A well balanced and refreshing drink.
5	**Martinez:** Very nineteenth century in its velvety sweetness, but well balanced because the gin isn't overly sweet. The bitters pull everything together into a rich briary/herb/root combination. Excellent.

BOTANICALS

Juniper • Cinnamon • Coriander seeds • Clove • Orange peel

BATHTUB OLD TOM GIN

42.4% UK

After the success of a gin allegedly made in his bathtub (*see* p.62), Professor Ampleforth continued in his explorations of gin history and at the suggestion of The Handmade Cocktail Company decided to re-create an Old Tom-style beverage. Once again, the technique of cold compounding has been used. The nose indicates sweetness, with some juniper and a fair whack of clove. The palate is quite thick and needs time to relax and open. There is considerably more cinnamon in the mouth than on the nose, and it becomes a little cloying on the finish. Water helps to lighten things, but the slightly medicinal clove note continues and the finish remains overly sweet. It's perhaps more of a liqueur gin than an Old Tom.

3.5 **G&T:** It works well on the nose, that sense of depth and sweetness working against the dry aspects of the tonic. A pleasant, sweet G&T.

4 **Gin Fizz:** This works well as long as you're careful with the sugar - the gin has enough. Get it right and there is a balancing act with the edgy lemon and the sugary gin. This has a certain verve.

4 **Martinez:** This gin was made to act as the base of a Martinez and it comes through well with cinnamon and clove. The bitters make it more savoury. If it's too sweet, reduce the vermouth levels and add another dash of bitters.

BOTANICALS

Juniper • Orange peel • Lemon peel • Coriander seeds • Cardamom • Angelica root • Aged in 100 per cent French oak wine barrels for 3–6 months

RANSOM OLD TOM 44% ABV USA

Sheridan, Oregon's Ransom Spirits was founded by Ted Seestedt in 1997 as a producer of grape-based spirits. He branched out into wine, then came whiskey, vodka, and, in 2009, gin. But not any old gin. Underpinning Seestedt's spirits is an appreciation of history and so he worked with his buddy, writer, and cocktail historian David Wondrich (*see also* p.181). For the latter, what was missing in gin was a liquid that could accurately re-create the spirit used in the first age of gin cocktails, which were built upon Hollands or Old Tom (*see* p.23). The base spirit is malt, and the botanicals are steeped in corn spirit, then distilled in a direct-fired still. Old Tom would also have been aged – for as long as it took to get to market – so this gin goes into oak until it gains the correct character. It's big, slightly yeasty, and rich, with medium levels of sweetness, floral notes, light oak, marmalade, high-flying spices, and candied peels. The palate is creamily rich and powerful, with the botanicals nearly encased. Cardamom and juniper show more distinctly as it opens with water. Off-dry and integrated, this is a class act.

4	**Gin Cocktail:** A complex nose with clove, angelica, orris, and coriander seeds. The bitters are a little too prominent on the end of the drink.
5	**Gin Fizz:** The gin absolutely flies here, showing its full complexity. Only a little sweetening needed. A real slinger.
5*	**Martinez:** This is the drink the gin was made for. The oak gives structure; the mix is complex, balanced, and layered, with a robust and hearty elegance. Glorious.

BOTANICALS

Juniper • Coriander seeds • Bitter orange peel • Angelica root • Grains of paradise • Cassia bark • Orris root • Cardamom • Tasmanian pepperberry • Aged for 6 months in ex-bourbon casks

BOURBON BARRELED BIG GIN 47% ABV USA

Coming from the new traditionalists Captive Spirits in Seattle (*see* p.139), this gin has spent a six-month period in ex-bourbon casks, which have had a very light impact on it, just sufficient to give little more than a suggestion of vanilla and a light grind of nutmeg. As well as that spicier nature, there also seems to be even more citrus here, with juniper being scaled back a bit from the standard bottling. The palate is very clean and has no aggression, and is not just a corn-based spirit but cask-mellowed. Only now does it move into a juniper forest with a twist of pepper. It needs a drop or two of water (or ice) to make a pleasant apéritif. It also works excellently with ginger ale, the *sec* extending and sweetening the finish.

3.5	**Gin Cocktail:** More vanilla comes through now. The spirit remains creamy and calm to start and then heats up into pepper flakes on the end.
3.5	**Gin Fizz:** The nose works well because of the light, creamy edge cutting through the lemon and soda. The roots have a part to play on the palate. A fair quick drink.
4	**Martinez:** This needs to be shifted up to a Turf Club ratio to let the gin come through. Now the juniper and pepper have a chance to add edge to the vermouth.

BOTANICALS

Juniper • Coriander seeds • Liquorice root • Orris root • Seville orange peel • Lemon peel • Bitter almond • Angelica seeds and root • Rested in ex-Jean de Lillet casks made of French oak

BURROUGH'S RESERVE OAK RESTED GIN 43% ABV UK

Created by Desmond Payne in 2013, Burrough's Reserve uses the standard Beefeater recipe (*see* p.63), but then the gin is given a period resting in Jean de Lillet casks. The wood influence is not too prominent – just enough to impart a straw colour – but it has acted as a vehicle for mellowing, lightly oxidizing and sweetening the flavours (Jean de Lillet is Sauternes-based). The classic Beefeater elements of citrus and juniper are there, but the effect is considerably more subtle and drifts the aromatics into Yellow Chartreuse (in which angelica is a big player) territory, with a slight floral, apricot note. The palate is clean with a little heat, and it does need water or an ice cube to calm it down – which is also a perfect way of drinking it; ginger ale works as well. It's balanced and elegant in the mouth, with a slightly sweeter edge and then a gingery, dry finish with more roots and juniper.

5	**Gin Cocktail:** The bitters meld in prettily, seemingly pulling out more Lillet notes. The gin remains subtle and clean. Soft and rather sophisticated.
3.5	**Gin Fizz:** Clean and fresh with good energy and the gin adding a little weight. The wood isn't too obtrusive, but it's not quite balanced.
5	**Martinez:** Rich and sweet, with fruity depths and mulled notes alongside an added biscuity edge. A quiet drink in a gentleman's club in the evening.

BOTANICALS

Juniper • Almond • Orris root • Fennel seeds • Aniseed • Grains of paradise • Orange peel • Cardamom • Violet root • Lemon peel • Coriander seeds • Cubeb berries • Cassia bark • Liquorice root • Savory • Nutmeg • Angelica root • Cumin seeds • Cinnamon • Aged first in a mix of ex-Cognac, Pineau des Charentes, and American oak, then married in a solera vat

CITADELLE RÉSERVE 2013

44% ABV France

After five years of experimentation, Citadelle's master distiller Alexandre Gabriel has finally decided on the formula for his aged expression (*see also* p.118). From the 2013 release onwards, Réserve will be different again. Gabriel is now using an adapted solera method in which the gin is split into three parcels, each of which is then aged in either American oak, ex-Pineau des Charentes, or ex-Cognac casks. After this, it is transferred to the solera vat, which is never emptied. When a bottling is made, the vat will be topped up with more gin from the next lot of casks to be filled. This gives consistency, more mellowing, and perhaps more volume. The effect is an intense spiced aroma with more menthol, balsam, and pepper than the non-aged version. The wood is restrained and the juniper has been softened. With water the coriander and peels kick in massively, while on the palate you get gentle, oozing pine, herbs, and powdery spices.

4	**Gin Cocktail:** Angelica comes through with some warm pepperiness, even peppermint, clove, and juniper. Scented. Becomes very peppery.
4	**Gin Fizz:** Light and restrained. The gin has had a calming effect with more violet, lavender, herbs, and pepper.
5	**Martinez:** Now there is an almost smoky edge, and though the gin remains subtle, it steers everything. Massive concentration on the mid-palate. Classic.

DUTCH COURAGE AGED GIN 88 44% ABV Netherlands

A newer arrival to Patrick van Zuidam's ever-growing range (*see also* pp.119 and 150), this came out in 2014. Here, the oak is a more active participant than is often the case in these gins, adding some charred notes and vanilla to the nose. This mix of the cask and malty spirit then adds in vibrant Chartreuse-type aromatics: aniseed, cardamom, and angelica alongside menthol and pine. The oak is prominent but not dominant. Water makes it more vanillic on the nose with some fresh-sawn timber – think of a new sauna – and shifts the aroma into an off-dry area, before the spices crunch down. The palate fights back against the oak with a big, spiced hit and acidity from the citrus, before it mellows into clove, aniseed, juniper, and coriander. Good on its own – treat it like a whisky. The issue is, will the mixes control the oak?

BOTANICALS

Juniper • Orris root • Coriander seeds • Angelica root • Sweet orange peel • Fresh whole lemons • Liquorice root • Cardamom • Vanilla pod • Aged for 9 months in new American oak

4	**Gin Cocktail:** The sweetness is the key here, as it softens the tannins and pulls down any aggressive elements, the bitters just adding to the mix. Light coconut.
X	**Gin Fizz:** The lemon doesn't like oak it would seem.
3.5	**Martinez:** Still slightly oak-driven with a firm palate, though the vermouth struggles to calm it down. As some tricky ratios are needed here to bring everything into balance, it's easiest to have it with ice or in a gin cocktail.

BOTANICALS

Juniper • plus 28 more • Aged for 4 months in Limousin oak

FILLIERS DRY GIN 28 BARREL AGED 43.7% ABV Belgium

Four months in cask is what it takes to change Filliers's standard 28 (*see* p.120) into this straw-yellow gin. The bouquet remains complex, though there has been a softening and mellowing of the spice attack. In addition, there seems to be more of a liquorice note, and an increase in lemon. The gentle oxidation has added weight. While the standard becomes dry with water, this turns more honeyed and heavy; you can imagine that you are in a spice shop in the seventeenth century. The palate shows a different structure with some wood-tightening effect, while still allowing the top notes and that creamy, rounded element to show. Water brings out more juniper and the finish is almost vermouth-like.

4	**Gin Cocktail:** The oak shows, but has botanical energy. Fresh yet long. Very worthwhile.
4	**Gin Fizz:** Quite rich and expressive, with some menthol along with citrus. Not hugely long, but classy.
5*	**Martinez:** Too sweet as a Martinez, but as a Turf Club you can see the elegance of the gin and the complexity of the botanical mix much better. Becomes a very sophisticated gin Manhattan – which is equally good at room temperature.

BOTANICALS

Undeclared but chosen from a selection of 2 classic and 13 from the Cape fynbos flora

INVERROCHE AMBER

43% ABV South Africa

Made with a different botanical mix of fynbos than Inverroche Classic (*see* p.125), this is not, despite the (yes, amber) colour, aged. Some of the fynbos botanicals have, however, been selected because of their tannin levels, which add colour and structure. They will also have been added post-distillation. In other words, while there is no oak, it behaves like a cask-aged gin, hence its inclusion here. There is a little camphor, a pleasant gloss paint note, and a sense of it all being quite sweet and polished: barley sugar, fruit sugars, and almost phenolic additions from the botanicals. It needs water, which makes it hugely perfumed. This carries through onto the palate, where this mix of wild herbs, patchouli, and fruit juice is reminiscent of walking into a hippy shop.

3	**Gin Cocktail:** A massive herbal burst with added clove and a little citrus. Moves more into a world of strawberry chews and bubblegum. Slightly odd.
3.5	**Gin Fizz:** The nose works, with the lemon and soda putting a brake on its boisterousness. The palate has retained the bubblegum/patchouli thing and adds a note of fresh lychee. It certainly has something.
3.5	**Martinez:** Very intense, even becoming more Negroni like, although there is no Campari involved. Highly citric with wild herbs flying around. The palate retains the confected element. I quite like it for all its unhinged madness.

BOTANICALS

Juniper • Coriander seeds • Cardamom • Lemon peel • Black peppercorns • Orange peel • Angelica root • Aged 50 per cent in ex-bourbon barrels, 50 per cent in ex-Old Scout bourbon barrels

SMOOTH AMBLER BARREL AGED 49.5% ABV USA

A product of Greenbrier Valley, West Virginia and made by TAG Galyean and John Little, this is based on a mash bill of corn, wheat, and barley malt that has been quadruple distilled in a pot/column hybrid still. The botanical mix looks relatively normal for an LDG (bar the pepper), but as this is a New Western-style gin (*see* p.138), the juniper plays a lesser role. The spirit is bottled straight as Greenbrier gin, but this version has then been aged in either ex-bourbon barrels or casks that previously held the firm's Old Scout bourbon. This moves the Greenbrier's estery sweetness into a more overtly herbal area. The cask has a decent say in proceedings, adding to the sweetness and giving a caramelized touch as well. Like most cask-aged gins, the citrus is also more prominent. On the tongue there is a light sweetcorn element from the spirit, while the oak shows a piney dimension. It's sweet and quite thick with eucalyptus, some oak, and herbs.

2.5 **Gin Cocktail:** This becomes very fruity and the oak notes add their piney quality as well as some coconut. More cask-influenced.

2.5 **Gin Fizz:** It should work, but again there is a clash with the wood here that knocks the lemon off balance.

3.5 **Martinez:** A spirited nose with light oak, but here the wood gives edge and style. The maraschino is more upfront with the vermouth playing a supporting role. Long with pleasing dustiness, while the finish has a savoury edge.

BOTANICALS

Juniper • Coriander seeds • Angelica root • Orris root • Lemon peel • Orange peel • Star anise • Cassia • Rose petals • plus 1 secret ingredient • Aged in French and American casks with added wood chips

VICTORIA OAKEN GIN

45% ABV Canada

The team at Victoria Spirits on Vancouver Island (*see also* p.134) take a slightly different approach in imparting wood notes to their Oaken Gin. A mix of small casks are used, to which wood chips are also added. This significantly increases the amount of contact the gin has with wood, effectively speeding up the extraction. The gin has broadened as well as mellowed, and while there is no loss of botanical influence – it's still clearly a gin – there is a new vanilla edge that has been absorbed, although not to the detriment of the pine and lemony warmth from juniper and coriander. On the palate there is a move towards aniseed with the dustiness of nutmeg and cinnamon. With water things are calmer but also creamier, with coconut and a charred element.

3.5	**Gin Cocktail:** Fresh and more citric, with the bitters adding a scented clove-like edge. Still rich and with good balance.
X	**Gin Fizz:** Goes all cream soda on you with a big aniseed hit. Slightly odd.
3.5	**Martinez:** Big botanical lift takes this into the realm of old-fashioned cough medicine with masses of cherry stone. Big, rich, and pretty sweet, so to get the gin influence, try as Turf Club.

BOTANICALS

Juniper • Coriander seeds • Lemon peel • Orange peel • Angelica seeds • Orris root • Fennel seeds • Saffron

BOUDIER SAFFRON GIN

40% ABV France

Gabriel Boudier is a long-established Dijon-based liqueur house (founded in 1874), run by the Battault family. Until 2008 it was best known for its crème de cassis, a ubiquitous presence on back bars. Then came Saffron Gin. Not wishing to produce a London Dry in France, Jean Battault let his mind go for a wander. In his opinion, there was a natural accord between juniper and saffron, backed up by the fact that in the firm's archive was a recipe for a saffron gin. Saffron might be an unusual ingredient today, but it was a vital one in Irish and Scottish *usquebaugh* from the seventeenth century onwards. In the nineteenth century, there was a French version known as *scubac*, which could be Boudier's original, but the firm isn't telling.

The colour glows (the saffron is added post-distillation), almost moving into the Day-Glo of a 1970s lava lamp. The saffron's honeyed element is present, but not overwhelmingly so; you can still pick out juniper, lemon, and coriander. The palate remains dry, with a little prick of orange, a touch of violet, some mint, and a floral edge. It's actually pretty classical in structure, with the fatness of saffron only coming across on the end. Is it a flavoured gin? Not in the same way as the fruit gins here, but where else does it go?

4.5	**With Tonic:** This works nicely. Heavier dilution brings some coriander, saffron, cut peels, fruit gums, and juniper. Saffron adds bulk to a lovely palate, then moves it into cooked orange. It may be just a little short, but a good and unusual apéritif.
X	**Gin Fizz:** Not applicable.

BOTANICALS

Juniper • Coriander seeds • Citrus peel • Angelica root • Orris root • plus Infused with heather and milk thistle and Perthshire raspberries

EDINBURGH GIN'S RASPBERRY LIQUEUR

20% ABV Scotland

Scotland is one of the foremost producers of soft fruits in Europe, with raspberries being the largest of the crops. No surprise then that when Alex Nicol was thinking of adding a fruit gin to his range (*see* p.81) he headed north to Perthshire and began harvesting. The berries are macerated with the standard Edinburgh gin and a judicious amount of cane sugar, and left to mature. It's immense and sweet, and reminiscent of homemade raspberry jam. The gin behind offers up a grind of pepper (I know it's normally added to strawberries, but it works here) and some juniper, and as it has a raspberry leaf element to it normally, it's an ideal match. The effect is really quite decadent when taken neat – as most people do. The palate starts refreshingly off-dry, pulsating with fruit and not too spirity. The sweetness kicks in again on the finish, making it just slightly cloying, but chilling helps.

4.5	**With Tonic:** It turns it into a very cool summer drink. The sweetness is cut by the tonic, while the fruits now show some slight acidity that cuts through and adds to the general perkiness.
4.5	**Gin Fizz:** Works very well indeed, with enough sweetness to carry. The raspberries come brimming out, the lemon adds acidity, and I can't help dreaming of "the hissing of summer lawns".

BOTANICALS

Undeclared but include Herefordshire damsons

FOXDENTON DAMSON GIN

18.5% ABV England

The Foxdenton Estate has been in the Radclyffe family since 1367 and is currently run by Nicholas Radclyffe. Like many country estates it has long been a centre for field sports. And what could be a better pick-me-up on a day's shooting than a fortifying sip from a hip flask of fruit gin? What started as a kitchen-made speciality for guests has now become another income stream for Nicholas. As well as a range of fruit liqueurs, there is also a gin (made by Charles Maxwell at Thames Distillers – *see also* pp.79, 82, 84, 93, and 105) and a range of fruit gins. The standard gin is a decent LDG, but the fruit gins are where the estate stands out from the crowd. The damsons are, in Nicholas's words, obtained "from a lovely lady in Herefordshire who grows them along her farm tracks". There is something of a home-cooked damson pie about this; it has density, depth, and the slightly sour tart bite that stops it just being sugar and fruit essence. The juniper then links into a mysterious, old aroma and the palate shows that it's not overdosed, the fruit's acidity giving it balance. This grown-up fruit gin comes highly recommended whether you have a gun in your hand or not.

5*	**With Tonic:** The pie filling is now oozing over the pastry. A classic, ripe, sweet/off-dry fruit gin that holds well across the palate, the tonic just giving sufficient effervescence. It also makes an awesome Wibble (*see* p.192). A drink for all the year.
5	**Gin Fizz:** Rich and deep with great colour. It has retained richness, the lemon just giving a bite to the soft fruits. A proper drink.

BOTANICALS

Undeclared but known to include:
Juniper • Cardamon • Coriander seeds • plus Wild, hand-harvested sloes

BRAMLEY AND GAGE ORGANIC SLOE GIN

26% ABV England

Put it down to nominative determinism – you know, having a surname that seems to preordain what your profession will be. If your names are Edward Bramley Kain and Penelope Gage, there really is only one business you should be in: fruit farming. The husband and wife team began making fruit liqueurs in their Devon kitchen in the 1980s. Sloe gin – the classic English fruit liqueur, although people never think about it like that – was not far behind. Today, the next generation of Kains is in charge of a considerably larger business, but the same principles of using whole fruits grown outdoors in Britain with no preservatives or colourings remains. This organic sloe gin, for example, only uses hedgerow-harvested fruit and has a higher sloe-to-gin ratio than B and G's standard expression (*see* p.59). The gin base itself is a secret, but chances are it will be close botanically to their 6 o'clock brand. It's lighter in colour than some and not as sweet either, allowing an intense sloe character to come across with cherry, violet, and that wild sour-berry edginess. The gin kicks in halfway through with lots of lavender and juniper, even a hint of angelica; classically bittersweet.

4.5 **With Tonic:** The mixer accentuates that acidity, making the combination less sweet and almost paradoxically more powerful as the gin begins to show its hand. Retains its bittersweet essence.

3.5 **Gin Fizz:** On slightly less sure ground, as the sloe and the lemon don't get along too well.

BOTANICALS

Juniper • Coriander seeds • Angelica root • Liquorice root • Orris root • Almond • Cassia bark • Cinnamon • Seville orange peel • Lemon peel • plus Wild sloes

SIPSMITH SLOE GIN 29% England

As you would expect from a distiller who has explored the history and traditions of gin, there is no great surprise that Jared Brown has created a fruit gin whose strength is almost 10 per cent higher than most. The effect doesn't make this spirity in any way, rather it adds an elegant, rich, and, dare I say, Victorian velvety richness to the nose. Wild sloes are steeped in Sipsmith's "standard" LDG (*see* p.107) and given light sweetening. Crimson in hue, the nose has touches of blackcurrant, black cherry, and then hints of pine and some sweet spice. The gin's texture adds weight to the palate. The latter shows massive levels of fruit, with a thrilling dark, bittersweet edge that flirts with being stewed, then pulls away before it gets too jammy. It's dense and wooded, like something you would be sipping nervously as you headed into an enchanted forest to rescue Little Red Riding Hood; complex in other words.

5	**With Tonic:** Rich, long, and autumnal. The mid-palate is opulent, and as the fruit falls off just before the finish, some ginny rootiness shows.
5	**Gin Fizz:** Berry fruits galore with pleasing sweetness to start, then it sours rather thrillingly. These elements then play off each other. A very adult drink.

BOTANICALS

Juniper • Coriander seeds • Chamomile • Elderflower • Citrus peels • Thai blue ginger • Cinnamon • Orris root • Elderberry • plus Beach plums

GREENHOOK GINSMITHS BEACH PLUM GIN LIQUEUR

30% ABV USA

Many of today's gin distillers share the same mindset as bartenders and chefs – when looking for flavours, they start in their immediate environs and see what can be foraged. The local is important to Brooklyn's Greenhook Ginsmiths, so when they decided to make a fruit gin, they sought out the New York equivalent of tart, bitter sloe berries. They found it in *Prunus maritima*, the mad little bittersweet plums that grow, mostly wild, along America's northeastern seaboard. The plums are small and tricky to pluck, but a source has been found in Long Island. These are then macerated in the firm's gin (*see* p.143). The fruits add an intriguing, almost medicinal edge that takes you back to old-style remedies, before they become more stewed with the bitter marzipan bite of stone. There is a fair hit of gin in here, with juniper proving to be the plums' main ally. It seems a little tense in the centre and maybe could do with a bit more sugar to balance, but that's a minor issue.

X	**With Tonic:** Becomes citric to start, but the plum notes are lost and it ends up a little short.
3.5	**Gin Fizz:** This is better, but there is still a slight separation between the spirit, the fruits, and then the lemon. Upping the sugar helps to add weight and length.

BOTANICALS

Undeclared • Aged in American oak

FILLIERS 1992 VINTAGE GRAANJENEVER, FIRST RELEASE 43% ABV Belgium

Filliers, the Belgian jenever (as it's spelled in Belgium) specialist, was founded in 1792 by farmer Karel Lodewijk Filliers, and remains under family ownership today. Their modern distillery, which was opened in 2006, produces jenever both for the family's own brands and for third parties in Belgium and Holland. Although the firm likes to keep their cards close to their chest, it is known that the mash bill for this 100 per cent grain jenever has a high rye content. It has also been aged for a decade in American oak. It's the rye rather than the wood that comes across most on the nose, with fresh, spicily sweet rye-bread notes and a hint of vanilla, before the light botanicals come through – fence posts, lemon, apple blossom, and butteriness. It's complex stuff. The palate confirms that it's distillate- rather than cask-driven, with a racy lemon acidity. It needs a drop of water to open up the rye notes and speed the silky texture.

5	**Gin Cocktail:** Take me back to New Amsterdam! This is maybe more refined than in pioneering nineteenth-century bartender Jerry Thomas's days (see p.26), but trust me, it's equally dangerous. You can never have just the one.
3.5	**Gin Fizz:** The acidity experienced when neat works against it slightly here. Fresh and with a bite.
4	**Martinez:** Even at Turf Club levels, this remains a very sweet drink, though the finish spices things up. Needs to be cold, cold, cold.

BOTANICALS

Juniper

BOLS GENEVER 42% ABV Netherlands

The Bulsius family were part of the sixteenth-century exodus of Flemish Protestants. In 1575, they arrived in Amsterdam, started distilling, and changed their name to Bols (*see* pp.12–13). The first account of juniper being purchased was by Pieter Bols in 1664 and by the seventeenth century, Bols's links with the Dutch East India Company resulted in the firm becoming a specialist in spiced liqueurs as well as genever. Recipes were gathered together in 1842 by the firm's then owner Gabriël Theodorus van 't Wout, and his *Distillateurs- en Liqueurbereiders Handboek door een oude patroon van 't Lootsje* (*Distillers and Liqueur-Makers Handbook by an old patron of "The Little Shed"*) is now in the Bols archive. One of its recipes, from 1820, is for this style of genever. Launched in 2008, it was the start of Bols's strategy of reclaiming cocktails for genever. It contains a blend of over 50 per cent malt wine and a juniper distillate, and is unaged. Clear and bright, it's lightly nutty with floral rye spice, a mellow draff note, and hints of citrus. The botanical influence is low. The palate is akin to a sweet new-make whisky, with a scented centre where the juniper lurks. Lightly oily, a very gentle spiciness comes across on the end.

4	**Gin Cocktail:** The bitters add their clove-like exoticism to all of these flowery, spring-like green notes. A simple drink, but a good one.
4	**Gin Fizz:** The genever stands up well here, adding a level of softness with a herbal edge to what is meant to be (and is) a sharp, shocking sling.
3.5	**Martinez:** The vermouth gives a big hit here, so I'd go to Turf Club levels, which adds earthy richness. Bitters provide a necessary balance.

BOTANICALS

Undeclared

BOLS ZEER OUDE

35% ABV Netherlands

"Oude" in this instance doesn't mean an aged genever but one that has been made in the old (*oude*) style and helps to differentiate it from the neutral, young (*jonge*) style, which began to be made in the 1920s. The very light yellow tint either shows that it's been in vat or, more likely, has been tinted with spirit caramel.

This is light and quite sweet on the nose, with delicate citrus and a touch of fresh-baked bread. It needs water to bring out the full aroma and also spread of flavour, which builds in crisp spiciness. The botanicals are gentle, but in genever they perform a supporting rather than dominant role. The palate has clean, quite citric, acidity that balances the richness of the spirit. There is plenty of spice on the end with some berries moving into raspberry, then a rye note on the very end. It seems delicate but has some character.

3.5	**Gin Cocktail:** More of the spiciness coming through here with the addition of the clove-rich bitters. Off-dry and moreish.
4.5	**Gin Fizz:** Slightly sweeter, again with the lemon and genever working in consort. It's a little short on the palate, but the nose more than makes up for that. In due course (if you allow a fizz to have time), it opens up to buttery baking spice.
4	**Martinez:** Savoury, with fruit, spices, and nuts fizzing together. Clean and citric, with good fleshiness as a Martinez.

BOTANICALS

Juniper • Hops • Clove • Aniseed • Liquorice root • Ginger • plus 1 secret ingredient • Aged 18 months in Limousin oak casks

BOLS BARREL AGED

42% ABV Netherlands

Today, the Bols recipe for malt wine is a 47% ABV triple-distilled mash of equal parts corn, rye, and wheat. This is then blended with a neutral grain-based botanical distillate and a malt wine juniper distillate. The Barrel Aged (50 per cent malt wine) was launched in 2011 and is from an 1883 recipe. Aged in Limousin oak for 18 months, it gives an idea of what the genever base for gin cocktails would have been like. Straw in colour, it has a sweet, malty, almost golden-syrup note with delicate spices (nutmeg, aniseed), dandelion, and pastry. The palate is silky and rich, with white peach to start, then a light grip from oak with a frisson of spice on the end. It needs water, as well as time in the glass.

4	**Gin Cocktail:** It's extraordinary how such a simple addition can change a drink. Broader yet still soft and more complex, with allspice and clove.
4	**Gin Fizz:** Sweetness is working here alongside the lemon. Some complexity. A clean and hugely drinkable shot.
5	**Martinez:** Puts you into a dimly lit nineteenth-century bar. Light bittering with just enough sweetness. Best as a Turf Club. Elegant is the word.

BOTANICALS

Juniper • Liquorice root • Aniseed • Aged in fresh American oak

ZUIDAM SINGLE BARREL ZEER OUDE, 3 YEAR OLD

38% ABV Netherlands

Patrick van Zuidam's (*see also* pp.119, 150, and 159) approach to genever starts with using a thick mash that is fermented with selected yeasts for a minimum of five days. Distillation is in Holstein stills, whose bases sit in a water bath, which prevents any scorching. It's this combination of time, yeast, and reflux that helps promote the lighter, more elegant notes to the base malt wine, which accounts for 50 per cent of this genever. Ageing is in new American oak barrels, which has had a significant impact on the nose. There is masses of creamy vanilla/clotted cream, soft banana notes, clove, stewed pear, and light berry. If you had this blind, you would say it was a Canadian whisky. It's only the hint of botanicals on the back palate that suggests otherwise. It might be OTT for genever purists, but any category needs people to push the boundaries. It's at its best with a drop of water or a cube of ice.

X	**Gin Cocktail:** There is little change here to be honest, as the cask influence is so strong. A little more structure with the bitters, but really it's the same drink.
X	**Gin Fizz:** Still this huge cask influence, with the wood getting in the way.
X	**Martinez:** Again, we are in the barrelhouse. It's better than the other two mixes, but not a great cocktail. It is, however, a genever that must be tried.

BOTANICALS

Juniper • Liquorice root • Aniseed, but an incredibly small amount

ZUIDAM ROGGE 35% ABV Netherlands

Rogge is Dutch for rye, which was the original base grain for genever – just as it was for American whiskey. Some of Zuidam's rye comes from near Groningen, where it's been planted as part of a conservation plan for ortolans (a small bird so loved by French gastronomes that it's now endangered), and like all of the firm's grains, it has been ground by windmill. This is clean with light sourdough notes (the link between bakers and genever is a constant) that have been mellowed by oak, which here has a very gentle influence. Light spices, lemon, with some dried mint and faint sage, it has real complexity and vivacity. Water adds an elegance to this sweet/spice interface, with hot cross buns coming through once more. The palate is clean, dry, and with a crisp feel that then moves into clove. Water brings out more spirit weight. Excellent.

5*	**Gin Cocktail:** A complete extra dimension with the bitters, which just add to the layers of complexity. The shade of Jerry Thomas (*see* p.26) reaches out a hand for a bottle.
3.5	**Gin Fizz:** This makes the whole mix slightly more restrained with pepper galore. A clean, crisp drink.
4	**Martinez:** Dry and spicy, with clean rye notes coming through the vermouth, then it surges forward in the mid-palate. Excellent weight. The balance of the Martinez mix shows an elegant side to the rye's rumbustious nature.

BOTANICALS

Juniper • Liquorice root • Aniseed • Aged in new American oak

ZUIDAM OUDE, SINGLE CASK 10 YEAR OLD 38% ABV Netherlands

In the 1950s, Fred van Zuidam was a distiller for deKuyper and witnessed at first hand the rapid decline of the genever industry. Despite distilleries closing down, sales declining, and a young generation turning their back on the spirit, he believed that people would eventually come back to genever – especially aged examples. The fact that the family distillery has now expanded substantially shows that his hunch has paid off. Son Patrick is not only an expert in distilling but in oak, and is ushering in a new range of flavours to genever through his cask policy, which includes ex-sherry and new oak. Wood is an active participant in many of his genevers, not simply a background note. This example has spent a decade in a single American oak cask and its vanilla notes are prominent, sitting alongside malt, wild herbs, crab apple, larch, and then rye crispbread, mixed spice, and coconut water. Big, velvety, and sweet, the palate has masses of Bounty bars and white chocolate. It's genever, but not as you know it.

X	**Gin Cocktail:** The coconut dominates. I'd keep things straight/iced.
X	**Gin Fizz:** The same goes here.
3.5	**Martinez/Turf Club:** I wasn't holding out much hope for this, but the nose is fantastic, with the sweetness and coconut working in tandem while the bitters fly happily above. It's a massive drink, but works even better as a Boulevardier.

BOTANICALS

Undeclared • Aged in American oak

FILLIERS OUDE GRAANJENEVER, 8 YEAR OLD

50% ABV Belgium

Filliers jenevers (*see also* p.170) are based on a mash bill of rye, wheat, and corn, with barley malt being added for its enzymes. Although the family don't divulge their distillation techniques (or botanical mixes), you can tell from its name that this brand has been made in the "old" nineteenth-century style, entirely with grain spirit (the meaning of *graan*), which in turn indicates that no spirit from base ingredients like sugar beet has been used. Both the malt wine and the juniper distillate are aged in American oak casks for a minimum of eight years. It is relatively strong for a jenever, but well rounded and soft, with some baking spices and a clear, rich malt wine influence making the nose fat and almost yeasty. The palate shows classic richness with some soft fruits to start but the steeliness of rye in the centre. The botanicals are gentle and light, and there is extra creaminess when water is added. It evolves well in the glass.

3.5	**Gin Cocktail:** Be careful with the bitters here. Quite herbal with a light dustiness.
3	**Gin Fizz:** Clean and slightly yeasty with some weight, but the wood sets up a clash.
5	**Martinez:** If you make this as a Turf Club, then you have yourself a damned fine drink. Broad, rich, and deep, it becomes a decadent drink.

BOTANICALS

Including: Juniper • Aniseed • Ginger • Hops • Angelica root • Liquorice root • plus 1 secret ingredient • Aged in Limousin and American oak casks

BOLS CORENWYN

38% ABV Netherlands

Corenwyn (Bols is the only distiller allowed to use this spelling) is a genever that contains a minimum of 51 per cent malt wine, although distillers usually have considerably more; up to 20 grams of sugar per litre can also be added. In Bols's case, the malt wine content is high and from their standard mash bill distilled once in column and twice in pot. This is then aged in cask from between two and 10 years, giving the blender a wide range of bases to draw from. The blend is then completed with a juniper and botanical distillate. Golden in colour, this has more energy than the Barrel Aged (*see* p.173) and shows more of a fresh cereal character. The botanicals are very subtle, slightly green, and lemony, and the richness of the aroma suggests that some old bases have been used. With water it becomes more fragrant and complex, with hedgerow fruits, lemon, flour, and a steely quality in the centre, before a spice mix like cumin and coriander comes in on the end of the palate.

5	**Gin Cocktail:** The bitters create a real lift-off. The palate is clean and quite light, with spices and real freshness. A sophisticated apéritif.
X	**Gin Fizz:** The wood comes into play and butts heads with the lemon, making the mix slightly unbalanced.
4	**Martinez:** Herbal and highly botanical, the vermouth has a substantial presence, but the genever cuts through. This has good impact, the sweet-bitter juxtaposition working well. Some complexity.

BOTANICALS

Juniper • Liquorice root • Aniseed • Aged in oloroso sherry casks

ZUIDAM KORENWIJN 1999

38% ABV Netherlands

All of Zuidam's genevers (*see also* pp.174–6) are based on a mash bill of malted barley, corn, and rye, which is given a long temperature-controlled fermentation (a week in the Korenwijn's case) and then triple distilled in a Holstein pot still. A percentage of this malt wine is then redistilled with botanicals, blended back with the original distillate, some neutral grain spirit, and put into cask. This has a high malt wine content and, unusually for a genever, has then spent a decade maturing in two oloroso sherry casks. These provide classic notes of Christmas cake mix, light walnut, a little vanilla, and some ginger. The spirit is very pure with a thick, almost syrup-like palate that has light tannins from the cask. There is sultana and spice to finish.

4	**Gin Cocktail:** Sherry casks usually repel all boarders, but here the gin holds up well, while the bitters add an intense top note.
X	**Gin Fizz:** Lemon and sherry? Don't think so.
3.5	**Martinez/Turf Club:** The bitters are the main driver of a long and sweet mix. It's slightly odd but weirdly likeable. It also works not too badly as a Boulevardier. It's probably easier to sip it neat, though.

BOTANICALS

Juniper • plus 15 more

HERZOG G.I.N. 40% Austria

Siegfried Herzog is the latest generation of the Herzog family, who have been distilling on a 400-year-old estate in Saalfelden, Austria. The firm has built a high reputation for its fruit schnapps, but has recently begun to branch out into other spirits, such as gin. This isn't a genever, strictly speaking, but on tasting and mixing it performed considerably better when it was treated as one rather than as a dry gin, so it's ended up in this section. As gin widens its remit, so these new intermediate gins will grow in number, which can only be good. The nose offers some potter's wheel notes, then robust roots, allspice, mace, clove, and, in time, juniper. The spirit is quite fat and malty, putting it in the "Hollands" camp. The palate is soft with some fennel seed and a milky note lingering beside the juniper, before the spices come forward. It dries into gentian.

3.5	**Gin Cocktail:** Good spirit working well with the tropical edges of the bitters. Some sweetness matching the nutty weight of the spirit. Light lavender on the finish.
3.5	**Gin Fizz:** Still quite a malty base, but it has decent spread with clove, aniseed, and then lemon. A decent short drink.
3.5	**Martinez:** Slightly malty still, which isn't necessarily a bad thing, as this nuttiness adds a dry note and a textural element. Clean and balanced.

BOTANICALS

Juniper • Hops • Aged in American oak casks for 3 months

CHIEF GOWANUS 44% ABV USA

A joint venture from New York Distilling Company's head honcho Allen Katz (*see also* p.142) and scribe David Wondrich (*see* p.155), this is a re-creation of the type of gin that Dutch settlers would have made. It's named after the chief of the tribe of Canarsie Native Americans from whom the Dutch acquired what was to become Brooklyn. It's also the name of the canal running through the borough that has the distinction of being one of the most polluted waterways in the USA. The recipe, which was discovered by Wondrich in the 1809 book *The Practical Distiller* by Samuel McHarry, redistills a rye whiskey with juniper and hops. It's then rested for three months, to replicate the period of time it would have taken gin to be transported from distillery to outlet in those days. The nose is fresh, clean, and rye-dominant, with an acidic lemony edge that could be spirit or the hops; the effect is like walking through a wintery pine forest. Light antiseptic, allspice notes lead into sweetness before the crackling, peppery acidic side of rye comes in. The finish is as cool as the exhalation of a menthol cigarette.

3.5	**Gin Cocktail:** The bitters help out, adding top notes and moving things further into the left field. You need a little more sugar than normal to balance.
3.5	**Gin Fizz:** Leave it to dilute slightly in the glass rather than knocking it straight back, as this stops it kicking like a mule and allows some softness to develop in the middle.
4	**Martinez/Turf Club:** The aroma is like a rye and raisin bagel. Hugely spicy, this works well in any of the late-nineteenth-century gin cocktails.

COCKTAILS

The drinks world can be divided into two eras: BV and AV, Before Vodka and After Vodka. It is only when you begin to delve into old cocktail books from the end of the nineteenth century and the start of the twentieth century that you get an idea of quite how important gin was in those BV days. If you wanted to use a white spirit in a drink, gin – be it genever, Old Tom, or dry – was your weapon of choice.

Cocktails made gin and gin, it could be argued, made cocktails. Think about that for a second. What other spirit could imbue a mixed drink with such grace and aromatic breadth? Gin was the cornerstone of mixed drinks. It gave us the Martini and Negroni, for Pete's sake! Because of this, it was hard for me to make a selection of the best classic drinks. If your interest is piqued, then there are plenty of worthy tomes in the bibliography to satisfy your mixological desires.

This wasn't just an exercise in archival studies, however; it was just as difficult to make a choice from the modern gin twists that today's top bartenders kindly sent in. If you want evidence of gin's renaissance, then look no further.

RECIPE

dry gin

dry vermouth

lemon twist, to garnish

Stir the ingredients over ice and strain into a chilled cocktail glass. Garnish with a lemon twist.

VARIATIONS

Here are some precursors of the classic gin Martini:

BRADFORD À LA MARTINI

½ wine glass of Old Tom
½ wine glass of vermouth
3 or 4 dashes of orange bitters
peel of 1 lemon
medium-sized olive, to garnish

Shake all the ingredients, including the lemon peel, over ice and strain into a chilled cocktail glass. Garnish with a medium-sized olive.

From Harry Johnson's *Bartenders' Manual*, 1888.

THE MARGUERITE

⅔ Plymouth Gin (*see* p.104)
⅓ French vermouth
dash of orange bitters

Stir all the ingredients over ice and strain into a chilled cocktail glass.

From Thomas Stuart's *Fancy Drinks and How to Mix Them*, 1896.

MARTINI

The Martini isn't just a drink. It's a cultural signifier, a rite of passage, a weapon. It started life (probably) in the late 1880s as a variant of the Martinez, but no one knows who first made it, where it was made, or when. For cocktail historian David Wondrich, its birth is "hazy and contradictory", which sounds like most people after a couple of Alessandro Palazzi's devilishly potent ones in the bar of the Dukes Hotel, London.

What started off as a democratic division between dry vermouth and gin (Old Tom was widely used), the Martini became progressively drier as the twentieth century advanced, so that at its zenith in the 1950s it had evolved into a cold-eyed assassin. It was, as Lowell Edmunds points out in his magisterial study *Martini, Straight Up*, urban, male, patrician, a businessman's drink. There was no romance about the Martini; it was the liquid equivalent of one of Hitchcock's glacial blondes. Dave Brubeck's sax player Paul Desmond said he wanted his tone to sound like a dry Martini, and it does - pure, skeletal, and ever so slightly soulless.

Because of these conservative trappings, the Martini began to disappear from the 1960s onwards. With vodka in the ascendency, the gin Martini was virtually forgotten. It was as if in order to become popular again it had to die and be reinvented. In the 1990s, the revival began, firstly with a vodka base and all manner of additions ("Martini" in those days was another word for a white spirit drink in a cocktail glass) but with gin's renaissance it has re-emerged in classic form and also become slightly wetter.

When you drink a Martini, you inevitably become a bore because you are the only person who knows how to make it correctly. The Martini is yours in a way that no other cocktail can be. It sets you apart. It's a loner's drink. You see, the barman doesn't make a Martini; the customer does. What gin? What vermouth? What ratio? Twist, olive, onion, or a dash of brine to make things dirty? All the bartender does is have the ingredients at hand and await your instructions.

NEGRONI

It goes like this. In the 1920s, this chap called Count Camillo Negroni walks into Bar Casoni in Florence, Italy at *aperitivo* time. Now, before we go any further, let's just dwell on the fact that Italian drinking culture is so advanced that time is set aside to take a specific type of drink that will both relax you after a day's work and sharpen your appetite. That means the drink has to have freshness, acidity, and a bitter edge. My favourite, since you're buying, is the Mezzo e Mezzo made with equal parts of Nardini Rosso (an amaro-style vermouth) and Rabarbaro (a rhubarb liqueur) as served at the firm's eighteenth-century bridge bar in Bassano del Grappa. Anyhow, the Count was looking for a similar hit, and was offered an Americano – equal parts Martini Rosso and Campari, lengthened with soda. Whatever the reason, he wanted something harder, so out went the soda and in went a slug of gin. It was his drink, so it got his name.

For me, the finest is to be had at Star Bar in Tokyo, Japan, where owner/master Kishi-san uses gin from the freezer, the fridge, and the shelf, which creates an incredible 3-D textural experience on the palate. It's worth the price of the air fare, trust me.

Although you shouldn't mess with a classic, you can work out your own variations on the theme – different vermouths, different amari, the mix bottle-aged or cask-aged – but never stray too far from the idea of the holy trinity. After all, gin, vermouth, and Campari are the booze equivalent of the celery, onion, and carrot *soffritto* that lies at the heart of great European cooking.

The Negroni is more than the sum of its parts. The gin provides the aromatics and can, if you use the Star Bar technique, add extra texture, while the Campari lends a bitter/sweet/sour/citric element. The vermouth spans these two extremes: sweet, fruity, bitter, rooty and herbal. It creates Escher-like flavour bridges everywhere in your mind, forever looping back on each other, which is why the overall balance is so important. It's the king of drinks.

RECIPE

30ml (1fl oz) gin

30ml (1fl oz) Campari

30ml (1fl oz) sweet vermouth

orange twist, to garnish

Build the ingredients in an ice-filled rocks glass, stir, and garnish with an orange twist.

VARIATIONS

BEGINNER'S NEGRONI

25ml (⅘fl oz) Plymouth Gin (*see* p.104)
25ml (⅘fl oz) Gancia Bianco vermouth
25ml (⅘fl oz) Aperol
pink grapefruit twist, to serve

Stir the ingredients over ice and strain into a chilled coupette glass. Squeeze a pink grapefruit twist over the rim of the glass and discard.

With thanks to Hannah Lanfear.

BELFAST BASTARD

60ml (2fl oz) Tanqueray London Dry Gin (*see* p.110)
15ml (½fl oz) Combier Crème de Pamplemousse Rosé
15ml (½fl oz) Dolin Blanc vermouth
15ml (½fl oz) Campari
2 dashes of Regan's Orange Bitters No. 6
grapefruit twist, to serve

Stir all the ingredients over ice and strain into a chilled coupette glass. Spray a grapefruit twist over the surface and discard.

From Jack McBarry of The Dead Rabbit Grocery and Grog, New York.

Both recipes from Gaz Regan's *The Negroni.*

JOHN (TOM) COLLINS

Who knows what London's Limmer's Hotel was like in 1830? Yet three decades later, Captain Rees Howell Gronow recalled it as being "the most dirty hotel in London". Grubby though it may have been, Limmer's was also, according to Gronow, "frequently so crowded that a bed could not be obtained for any amount of money; but you could always get a very good plain English dinner, an excellent bottle of port, and some famous gin-punch". The gin punch had been the creation of Limmer's head waiter in the 1830s, a cove called John Collins who was famed for the quality of his libations. The one that would bear his name was a short, single-serve simple Gin Fizz – made with Old Tom – which cocktail historian David Wondrich believes would have been similar to the The Garrick Gin Punch (*see* p.190). It was so good that Collins even had a piece of doggerel written about his drink.

Like most of these proto-cocktails, this would have started life as an eye-opener and hangover cure. Limmer's "gloomy, comfortless coffee-room" was after all, according to Gronow, "where might be seen many members of the rich squirearchy, who visited London during the sporting season". We don't have gin for breakfast much these days – although the strange routine of writing a gin book does mean I had plenty of these at what polite society would consider a disgracefully early hour. I can vouch for their efficacy.

By the middle of the nineteenth century, the drink had jumped the Pond to America and by the 1870s had changed its name as well. John Collins had become Tom – maybe after Old Tom, maybe due to a mishearing. It had also been altered. The John Collins started off as a short, shaken Gin Fizz (*see* p.212). The Tom Collins used the same ingredients but became a longer drink, built over ice cubes and stirred. It also, in time, shifted from being an Old Tom drink to one made with dry gin. When you go back to its nineteenth-century roots and make this with Old Tom or *oude* genever (see p.172), it's a revelation – a drink with heft and richness, no matter what its name.

RECIPE

50ml (1¾fl oz) Old Tom gin or dry gin

20ml (⅗fl oz) fresh lemon juice

25ml (⅘fl oz) simple syrup or gomme (*see* below)

90ml (3fl oz) club soda

FOR THE GARNISH

orange slice

maraschino cherry

Shake the first 3 ingredients with ice and strain into an ice-filled Collins glass. Add the soda, stir, and garnish with an orange slice and a maraschino cherry.

SIMPLE SYRUP

Gently heat equal quantities of white sugar and water until the sugar has completely dissolved. You can flavour the syrup by adding mint leaves, citrus peel, and so on. Alternatively, just buy a bottle of gomme.

GIN PUNCH

Gin came slightly late to the punchbowl. Although there are records of hot gin punch being quaffed in London in the 1730s, gin was by then a low-class liquor (*see* pp.14–19). No self-respecting punch-drinking gentleman would be seen supping from a bowl of Mother's Ruin. They stuck to rum or brandy. By the late eighteenth century, however, things had started to change. Gin's quality was improving and it was acquiring a certain risqué cachet with London's bohemian set.

No surprise, then, that the first gin punch to achieve fame was that made at the Garrick Club, which had been established in 1831 in the West End of London as a place where "an easy intercourse was to be promoted between artists and patrons", a phrase that probably read slightly differently at the time than it does today. Its manager was an American, Stephen Price, and it was he, cocktail historian David Wondrich argues, who was the first to combine gin, ice, and carbonated water in a punch.

The fact that William Terrington listed eight gin punches in his 1869 book *Cooling Cups and Dainty Drinks* shows how gin punch's elevation was complete by the mid-nineteenth century (*see* pp.22–3). The final seal of approval was its regular appearance in the work of Charles Dickens (himself no mean gin lover), most famously in *A Christmas Carol*, where Bob Cratchit "turning up his cuffs... compounded some hot mixture in a jug with gin and lemons, and stirred it round and round and put it on the hob to simmer". As Terrington says:

> "...there is no precise rule for making punch, no two persons agreeing on the exact proportions of the ingredients... The great secret is that the mixture should be so happily compounded that nothing predominates."

His own variant, by the way, is the Garrick with Green Chartreuse taking the place of the Maraschino.

While in its element as a cooling and (fairly) dainty summer drink when fruit and soda water are the order

RECIPE

Serves 6

1 bottle of gin – try mixing Portobello Road (*see* p.105) and Hayman's Royal Dock (*see* p.91)

1 bottle of Madeira (Malmsey)

3 cloves

pinch of freshly grated nutmeg

2 cassia bark sticks

2 tsp demerara sugar

6 large lemon and orange twists

1 small orange slice

3 tbsp clear honey, plus extra to taste as needed

juice of 2 lemons, plus extra to taste as needed

Combine all the ingredients in a saucepan and heat gently. Cover and keep at a very gentle simmer for 20 minutes. Taste and adjust with honey and/or lemon juice. Strain into bowl and serve warm.

VARIATION

GIN PUNCH À LA HEPPLE

2 parts Hepple Gin
1 part Lemon and Seville Orange Sherbet (*see* below)
1 part fresh lemon juice
1 part pineapple syrup
3 parts chilled Sencha green tea
2 parts Prosecco or *demi-sec* Champagne

FOR THE LEMON AND ORANGE SHERBET
4 Seville oranges
6 lemons
250g (9oz) caster sugar

FOR THE GARNISH
borage flowers
lemon and orange wheels
pineapple sticks

To make the Lemon and Seville Orange Sherbet, grate the zest of the oranges and lemons, then squeeze 300ml (10fl oz) of juice from the oranges and an equal quantity of juice from the lemons. Muddle the citrus zests and sugar together, then add the citrus juices and mix until the sugar has dissolved – gently heat if necessary. Strain.

Mix the first 5 main ingredients together, then top up with the Prosecco or *demi-sec* Champagne. Garnish with borage flowers, lemon and orange wheels, and pineapple sticks.

With thanks to Nick Strangeway, Strangehill, London, who in turn was inspired by William Terrington.

THE GARRICK GIN PUNCH

Serves 8
1 lemon (or more if necessary to yield 90ml/3fl oz juice)
25g (1oz) caster sugar
60ml (2fl oz) Maraschino
230ml (8fl oz) gin (*oude* genever or Old Tom)
600ml (1 pint) water (either as water or as an ice block)
470ml (16½fl oz) soda water, chilled

Using a vegetable peeler or paring knife, peel the lemon, being careful to avoid the bitter white pith. Place the lemon peel in a bowl or pitcher. Squeeze the juice from the lemon and measure out 90ml (3fl oz). Add the sugar and Maraschino to the lemon peel and muddle well. Add the gin, lemon juice, and water or ice and stir well, then top up with the soda and serve.

From David Wondrich's *Punch*.

of the day to freshen the palate, gin punch also works in winter. Since the Victorians invented what we now think of as a traditional Christmas, it's only right that we should include a Dickensian-style warm punch – a sort of mulled gin – as part of the festivities. It is a lot easier to have a bowl of this to dispense, rather than rushing around trying to sort out a myriad different requests. If anyone complains, then you can retort in the manner of Fagin to Oliver, "Shut up and drink yer gin!"

THE BRAMBLE

RECIPE

40ml (1⅓fl oz) gin

20ml (⅗fl oz) fresh lemon juice

20ml (⅗fl oz) simple syrup or gomme (*see* p.188)

20ml (⅗fl oz) crème de mûre

blackberry, to garnish

Shake the first 3 ingredients with ice and strain into a highball glass filled with crushed ice. Dribble the crème de mûre down through the ice. Garnish with a blackberry.

VARIATION

For me, the Wibble is a better, more complex, grown-up version of the Bramble that amplifies the sweet and sour elements while adding layers of fruit. It was invented by Dick when he was at London's Soho bar, The Player, and named after the always erect Nick Blacknell, then marketing director of Plymouth Gin. As Dick said, "it will make you wobble, but you won't fall down".

THE WIBBLE

25ml (⅘fl oz) Plymouth Gin (*see* p.104)
25ml (⅘fl oz) Plymouth Sloe Gin*
25ml (⅘fl oz) fresh pink grapefruit juice
10ml (⅓fl oz) fresh lemon juice
5ml (⅙fl oz) simple syrup or gomme (*see* p.188)
10ml (⅓fl oz) crème de mûre

Shake all the ingredients with ice and strain into a chilled glass, with or without ice.

***Recently I've replaced the Plymouth Sloe Gin with Sipsmith Sloe Gin (*see* p.168) or, even better, Foxdenton Damson Gin (*see* p.166).**

Funny the tricks that the memory plays, especially when there is drink involved. How many great recipes have been lost in the mists of a 4am post-shift experimentation? Such is the case with the Bramble. What we *can* say is that it was created at some point in the late 1980s in a bar called Fred's in London's Soho. And it was definitely the work of Dick Bradsell, who manned the stick at that particular establishment, which itself was the underground haunt of disreputable bohemian classic cocktail lovers, or BCCLs, when such a thing was still, appropriately enough, underground.

It's easy to forget how hard it was to get a great drink anywhere outside of the grand hotels in those days, and since none of the BCCLs wore ties or jackets, they couldn't be served in most of those establishments anyway. The answer was to create your own scene. When that happened, Dick was its leading light. He is one of the very few bartenders to have three modern classics to his name – the others being the Espresso Martini and the Russian Spring Punch – in his lifetime.

But anyway, back to the Bramble. I seem to recall Plymouth being the gin that was used originally, but I suspect that is my mind playing tricks... certainly it was a time of excess. Maybe it's because it is the gin I would reach for, or perhaps I'm blurring the Bramble with the Wibble (*see* Variation), which of course is another of Dick's drinks. The man should have a statue erected in his honour – an underground statue, waving from a basement.

The important thing is that this works. That's why it's a modern classic. It refreshes, but the crème de mûre adds a sultry richness to the experience. It takes me back to fuzzy long evenings and happenings that best have a veil drawn quietly over them, but if we ever meet, let me tell you about the potato gun standoff in Louisville Airport.

RECIPE

30ml (1fl oz) Old Tom gin

20ml (⅗fl oz) Maraschino

15ml (½fl oz) fresh lemon juice

Shake all the ingredients with ice and strain into a chilled Martini glass.

AVIATION

When you glance at the recipe for the Aviation, you wonder what the fuss is about. It seems simple – too simple, perhaps, in the same way that jungles can be too quiet just before the enemy attacks. On paper, there is little more to this than a simplified single-serve Garrick Gin Punch (*see* p.190). It's a gin sour, it's a gin Floridita Daiquiri, and yet there is complexity lurking within. The trick, as ever with drinks with so few ingredients, is balance. The lemon juice needs to be fresh (of course), the Maraschino at just the right level, and the gin to have a suitably amenable complexity.

Let's have a look at the gin. The recipes say dry, but I would be more specific and go for a style like Plymouth (*see* p.104). Better still is Old Tom, as this gives the little touch of sweetness that is needed; this can be too sour otherwise. Hayman's works excellently (*see* p.153), as does Hammer & Son Old English (*see* p.152).

Maraschino and gin have a wonderful relationship. The liqueur was a speciality of Zadar in Croatia, though production post-World War Two switched primarily to the Veneto region of northeastern Italy. It first appeared in Britain in the 1770s, becoming a cult drink and a favourite of the aristocracy. In the days when people had fewer ingredients to play with, there is little surprise that it began being used in simple mixed drinks. Although a liqueur, it isn't too sweet and has an earthy note – which links with angelica and orris – along with a deep fruitiness that brings to mind roses, cherry pie (with slightly burned pastry), hay, and hill tracks. Overload things and it dominates, but get it right and your drink will fly, which is kind of appropriate.

Originally, the Aviation included crème de violette as well as Maraschino, which gave it a cerulean hue and a more floral edge. The colour alone would make it the perfect accompaniment to have in Ian Fleming's "violet hour", were you not drinking a Vesper. Whatever way you choose, this is another gin drink where it's hard to have just one.

RAMOS GIN FIZZ

Where would the world be without New Orleans drinks? – infinitely poorer, though probably slightly clearer-headed. Henry C Ramos (known to all as Carl) moved to the Crescent City in 1888 as the new owner of the Imperial Cabinet Saloon on the corner of Gravier and Carondelet, an establishment that would soon be called "the most famous gin fizz saloon in the world" by the *Kansas City Star*. In 1907, he moved further along Gravier to the Stag Tavern and took his drink with him.

Carl Ramos was the King of the Fizz, and he made his differently. His Gin Fizz didn't exactly fizz – it glided. It also took time to make, but in my experience people always have time in New Orleans. He took the basic Fizz recipe (*see* p.212) and dolled it up with cream, egg white, and orange flower water. As a result, it ceased to be a sharpener and instead became something luxurious. It took time because the key to the Ramos Gin Fizz is the length of the shake.

Carl, famously, had shaker "boys" (i.e. African Americans), up to six per barkeep, whose job was simply to keep on shaking. Some reports say that they kept on shaking even if they dozed off; others recount that as each shaker boy became tired he would pass the drink along to his neighbour, who would keep the agitation going until the drink was ready. How long was that, you ask? Charles H Baker (*see* Variation) said one minute, while others say three... or five... or more..., but let's hear it from Carl Ramos himself: "Shake and shake and shake until there is not a bubble left, but the drink is smooth and snowy white and the consistency of good rich milk."

There is a certain sadistic pleasure to be had in asking a hard-pressed bartender to make a round of them. Equally, if making at home and you have a smallish child, get them to shake it for you. They have to learn sometime. Some say you can make this in a blender, but that strikes me as low-down cheatin'.

RECIPE

45ml (1½fl oz) Old Tom gin

3–4 drops of orange flower water

juice of ½ lemon

juice of ½ lime

1 egg

2 tbsp single cream

1 tbsp icing sugar

30ml (1fl oz) soda water

Shake all the ingredients, bar the soda water, ferociously over crushed ice for a minimum of 2 minutes. The drink should have the consistency of single cream. Strain into a chilled cocktail glass and top up with the soda water.

VARIATION

Charles H Baker was a wealthy American dilettante who cruised around the world's finest temples to food and drink in the twenties and thirties, and his libationary recollections are a magnificent encapsulation of a forgotten age of cocktails. His Gin Fizz Tropical takes the Ramos basics and replaces sugar with pineapple syrup, the lemon juice with that from 1½ limes, and uses fresh mint for garnish. He drank it after running the Pagsanjan rapids in the Philippines: "a rocky gorge of towering walls hung with weird tropical growths, peopled with gibbering monkeys and vivid unnameable birds".

SINGAPORE SLING

Gin became the favoured drink of those Dutch and British empire builders who were posted to the East. Genever would have been drunk from the eighteenth century if you were Dutch, and although it took longer for British gin to shake off its low-class image (*see* p.20), by the nineteenth century it had become the ideal spirit to sip when taking your sundowner in British-ruled colonies, a habit that carried on through the twentieth century and, among the sensible, up until today.

A gin-based drink is perfect for those times when your forehead is beading with perspiration and your linen suit is losing its crispness. The best of them are deliciously, dangerously moreish. The night is young, and the heat has ceased to be oppressive and instead become like a silken blanket caressing your skin.

The greatest chronicler of this mode of drinking is Charles H Baker (*see* p.197), and the gin drink that best personifies it is that created in Singapore's Raffles Hotel. Baker says of "The Immortal Singapore Raffles Gin Sling":

> "There are other good Gin Slings in the East... but the Raffles drink is the best. When our soft-footed Malay boy brings the fourth Sling and finds us peering over the window sill at the cobra-handling snake charmers tootling their confounded flutes below, he murmurs 'Take care, master'. The Singapore Gin Sling is a delicious, slow-acting, insidious thing."

The problem is how to make it. It started, cocktail historian Ted Haigh attests, as the Straits Sling, but was soon sweetened (with cherry brandy replacing kirsch) – and lengthened, becoming more of a proto-tiki drink (the OTT fruity rum-based concoctions popular in the fifties).

As is often the case with famous drinks, their spiritual home often ends up being the place where the worst examples are made. Raffles's Singapore Sling was, in recent times, one of those. However, Desmond Payne, the guru of gin and a man who belongs on that hotel's terrace (*see* pp.64 and 157), reported in 2015 that it was back to its old standard. Mr Baker would approve.

RECIPE

30ml (1fl oz) gin

30ml (1fl oz) Cherry Heering

30ml (1floz) Bénédictine

30ml (1fl oz) fresh lime juice

60ml (2fl oz) soda water

dash of Angostura bitters

Build the first 4 ingredients in an ice-filled glass, then stir, top up with the soda water and add the bitters.

Baker notes that "in other parts drinkers often use ginger ale instead of soda, or even stone bottle ginger beer". His Sling also uses 2 parts Old Tom to 1 part cherry brandy and 1 part Bénédictine.

VARIATIONS

Also, check out the Pegu Club (*see* p.206).

THE STRAITS SLING

60ml (2fl oz) gin
15ml (½fl oz) kirschwasser
15ml (½fl oz) Bénédictine
juice of ½ lemon
2 dashes of orange bitters
2 dashes of Angostura bitters
soda water, to top up
fruits of your choice, to garnish

Shake all the ingredients, bar the soda water, over ice. Strain into a chilled sour glass or Champagne flute. Top up with soda and garnish with whatever fruits you fancy.

From Ted Haigh's book *Vintage Spirits and Forgotten Cocktails.*

THE BRONX

This was invented by Johnnie Solon at the Waldorf-Astoria Hotel in Manhattan, New York City, at the turn of the twentieth century.

60ml (2fl oz) gin

1½ tsp sweet vermouth

1½ tsp dry vermouth

30ml (1fl oz) fresh orange juice

orange bitters, to taste

orange twist, to garnish

Shake all the ingredients with ice and strain into a chilled cocktail glass. Garnish with an orange twist.

THE CLOVER CLUB (right)

Another early twentieth-century mix, which sadly fell from fashion (probably because of its pink hue) when mixed drinks were only for Real Men, but is returning to favour in these more metrosexual times.

40ml (1⅓fl oz) gin

15ml (½fl oz) simple syrup or gomme (*see* p.188)

20ml (⅗fl oz) fresh lemon juice

5ml (⅙fl oz) raspberry syrup

5ml (⅙fl oz) egg white

Shake all the ingredients with ice and strain into a chilled cocktail glass.

CORPSE REVIVER NO 2

As Harry Craddock (see p.28) wrote in his The Savoy Cocktail Book *of 1930, "four taken in quick succession will unrevive the corpse again". You have been warned.*

30ml (1fl oz) gin

30ml (1fl oz) Cointreau

30ml (1fl oz) Lillet Blanc vermouth

30ml (1fl oz) fresh lemon juice

absinthe, to taste (go easy)

Shake all the ingredients with ice and strain into a chilled cocktail glass.

From Ted Haigh's book *Vintage Spirits and Forgotten Cocktails*.

FRENCH 75 (left)

Although in New Orleans this is made with Cognac – appropriately enough, as it's named after a French field gun – this has always been a gin drink.

60ml (2fl oz) gin

30ml (1fl oz) fresh lemon juice

10ml (⅓fl oz) or 2 tsp simple syrup or gomme (*see* p.188)

Champagne, to top up

Shake the first 3 ingredients with ice and pour into a chilled Collins glass. Top up with Champagne.

THE FORD COCKTAIL

The use of Old Tom shows this to be a nineteenth-century classic – it dates from 1895.

30ml (1fl oz) Old Tom gin

30ml (1fl oz) dry vermouth

3 dashes of Bénédictine

3 dashes of orange bitters

orange twist, to garnish

Stir all the ingredients with ice and strain into a chilled cocktail glass. Garnish with an orange twist.

From Ted Haigh's book *Vintage Spirits and Forgotten Cocktails*.

ANGEL FACE MARTINI

25ml (⅘fl oz) Tanqueray No. TEN (*see* p.111)

25ml (⅘fl oz) Calvados

25ml (⅘fl oz) apricot liqueur

orange twist, to garnish

Stir all the ingredients together and then serve in a frozen coupe glass, garnished with an orange twist.

From Barrie Wilson, global brand ambassador, Tanqueray gin.

FAIRBANK COCKTAIL

This first appeared in Harry MacElhone's ABC of Mixing Cocktails *in 1922 and is named after the swashbuckling star Douglas Fairbanks.*

50ml (1¾fl oz) gin

20ml (⅗fl oz) dry vermouth

2 dashes of orange bitters

2 dashes of crème de noyaux

cherry, to garnish

Stir in a mixing glass with ice and strain into a chilled cocktail glass. Garnish with a cherry.

From Ted Haigh's book *Vintage Spirits and Forgotten Cocktails.*

GIMLET (right top)

Seemingly simple, yet tricky to manage. This needs to be COLD. Adding equal amounts of lime juice and cordial helps, or lengthen with soda.

50ml (1¾fl oz) gin

7.5ml (¼fl oz) fresh lime juice

7.5ml (¼fl oz) lime cordial

lime wedge, to serve

Shake all the ingredients with ice and strain into a chilled cocktail glass. Serve with a lime wedge.

HANKY-PANKY (right bottom)

This cocktail was first created in the 1920s by Ada Coleman, head bartender of The Savoy Hotel's American Bar, London, and named after actor Sir Charles Hawtrey (but not the one of Carry On *film fame).*

45ml (1½fl oz) gin

45ml (1½fl oz) sweet vermouth

2 dashes of Fernet-Branca

strip of orange peel, to serve

Stir all the ingredients with ice and strain into a chilled cocktail glass. Twist a swathe of orange peel over the surface of the drink.

MONKEY GLAND

One from Harry's New York Bar in 5 rue Daunou, Paris, guaranteed to revitalize parts that other drinks do not reach.

60ml (2fl oz) gin

20ml (⅗fl oz) fresh orange juice

1 tsp grenadine

1 tsp absinthe

Shake all the ingredients with ice and strain into a chilled cocktail glass.

ASTORIA BIANCO (right)

An offering from Jim Meehan of New York's PDT bar (see also *pp.211 and 216), who adds: "Years before Old Tom gin was reintroduced on the US market, I approximated the flavour profile by substituting bianco vermouth for dry in his resurrection of the Astoria cocktail."*

75ml (2½fl oz) Tanqueray London Dry Gin (*see* p.110)

30ml (1fl oz) Martini Bianco vermouth

2 dashes of orange bitters

orange twist, to garnish

Stir all the ingredients with ice and then strain into a chilled coupe glass. Garnish with an orange twist.

PEGU CLUB

A colonial delight, this was created as a sundowner for the denizens of Rangoon's (now Yangon) Pegu Club, Burma (now Myanmar), in the 1920s.

45ml (1½fl oz) gin

15ml (½fl oz) Cointreau

20ml (⅗fl oz) fresh lime juice

2 dashes of Angostura bitters

Shake all the ingredients with ice and strain into a chilled cocktail glass.

From Ted Haigh's book *Vintage Spirits and Forgotten Cocktails.*

THE VESPER

Invented by Ian Fleming, this features in Casino Royale, *the first James Bond novel, and was named after Bond's squeeze in the book, double agent Vesper Lynd. It was originally made with the now sadly discontinued Kina Lillet.*

90ml (3fl oz) gin

30ml (1fl oz) vodka

15ml (½fl oz) Lillet Blanc vermouth

lemon twist, to garnish

Shake all the ingredients with ice and strain into a chilled stemmed glass. Garnish with a lemon twist.

WHITE LADY (far right)

Another from the fertile mind of Harry MacElhone (see Fairbank Cocktail, p.204), this cocktail emerged in the Roaring Twenties in Paris. These days, it's most commonly seen being drunk in upscale bars in Tokyo.

40ml (1⅓fl oz) gin

20ml (⅗fl oz) fresh lemon juice

25ml (⅘fl oz) Cointreau

Shake all the ingredients with ice and strain into a chilled cocktail glass.

TWENTIETH CENTURY COCKTAIL (right)

Created in 1937, this cocktail was not named after the new century but the then newly designed Twentieth Century Limited train that ran between New York and Chicago.

45ml (1½fl oz) gin

15ml (½fl oz) Lillet Blanc vermouth

15ml (½fl oz) white crème de cacao

15ml (½fl oz) fresh lemon juice

Shake all the ingredients with ice and strain into a chilled cocktail glass.

BREAKFAST MARTINI (left)

40ml (1⅓fl oz) gin

20ml (⅗fl oz) fresh lemon juice

20ml (⅗fl oz) Cointreau

1 level tsp marmalade (no rind)

toast, to garnish

Shake all the ingredients with ice and strain into a chilled cocktail glass. Serve with toast.

From Salvatore "The Maestro" Calabrese of the Playboy Club, London.

SILVER FIZZ

First made in the 1880s in either New York or Chicago (debate rages), this was intended as an early morning picker-upper. I can vouch for its continuing efficacy.

50ml (1¾fl oz) gin

35ml (1⅙fl oz) simple syrup or gomme (*see* p.188)

25ml (⅘fl oz) fresh lemon juice

20ml (⅗fl oz) egg white

60ml (2fl oz) soda water

Shake the first 4 ingredients long and hard with ice. Strain into a chilled highball glass without ice and top up with the soda water.

AFTER NINE

This comes courtesy of Jim Meehan of PDT cocktail bar, New York City (see also *pp.206 and 216*), *who comments: "A fitting reward for a vigorous day on the slopes; this winter warmer also delights those of us who spend more time looking at mountains than scaling them."*

30ml (1fl oz) Monkey 47 Schwarzwald Dry Gin (*see* p.130)

240ml (8½fl oz) lavender mint tisane, freshly brewed

15ml (½fl oz) Marie Brizard Cacao Blanc

1½ tsp Chartreuse V.E.P. Verte (green)

sprig of lavender, to garnish

Build the ingredients in a pre-warmed insulated toddy mug. Garnish with a sprig of lavender.

CHOCOLATE NEGRONI

30ml (1fl oz) Fords gin (*see* p.84)

22ml (¾fl oz) Campari

22ml (¾fl oz) Punt e Mes red vermouth

5ml (⅙fl oz) white crème de cacao

2 dashes of chocolate bitters

orange twist, to garnish

Stir all the ingredients together, then strain into a chilled cocktail glass onto one large piece of ice. Garnish with an orange twist.

From Naren Young, Fork & Shaker, New York City.

HOUSE GIN FIZZ (right top)

50ml (1¾fl oz) London Dry gin

25ml (⅘fl oz) fresh lemon juice

10ml (⅓fl oz) extra virgin olive oil

20ml (⅗fl oz) simple syrup or gomme (*see* p.188)

25ml (⅘fl oz oz) egg white

pinch of vanilla salt

soda water, to top up

lemon twist, to garnish

"Dry" shake (without ice) all the ingredients, bar the soda, together, then repeat with ice. Strain into a chilled sling glass with no ice. Top up with a splash of soda and garnish with a lemon twist.

From Ryan Chetiyawardana of White Lyan, Hoxton, London.

START ME UP (right bottom)

45ml (1½fl oz) gin

10ml (⅓fl oz) apricot brandy

5ml (⅙fl oz) aquavit

5ml (⅙fl oz) sugar syrup or gomme (*see* p.188)

20ml (⅗fl oz) peach-infused Cocchi Americano

lemon twist, to garnish

Stir all the ingredients over ice and strain into a chilled cocktail glass. Garnish with a lemon twist.

From Rob Libecans of White Lyan, Hoxton, London.

JASMINE (left)

45ml (1½fl oz) gin

20ml (⅗fl oz) Combier triple sec

15ml (½fl oz) Campari

20ml (⅗fl oz) fresh lemon juice

15ml (½fl oz) simple syrup or gomme (*see* p.188)

pansy flower, to garnish (optional)

Shake all the ingredients together and fine strain into a cocktail glass. Garnish with a pansy, if available.

From Naren Young, Fork & Shaker, New York City.

AU THÉ VERT

50ml (1¾fl oz) Tanqueray London Dry Gin (*see* p.110)

25ml (⅘fl oz) fresh lemon juice

20ml (⅗fl oz) Oak Moss Syrup (*see* below)

½ tsp Bénédictine

dash of orange blossom water

75ml (2½fl oz) Jasmine Tea (*see* below)

seasonal edible flowers – jasmine blossom if available, to garnish

FOR THE OAK MOSS SYRUP

50g (2oz) oak moss

2kg (4½lb) sugar

1 litre (1¾ pints) water

FOR THE JASMINE TEA

25g (1oz) jasmine loose leaf tea

125ml (4fl oz) water at 90°C (194°F)

125ml (4fl oz) cold water

For the oak moss syrup, put all the ingredients into a saucepan and heat until the sugar dissolves. Remove from the heat and leave to infuse for an hour, then strain through a Superbag strainer. Pour into a sterilized bottle, seal, and date, then stick in the fridge. It will keep for a month.

To make the jasmine tea, brew the tea in the hot water for 4 minutes. Add the cold water and quickly strain. Pour into a sterilized bottle, seal, and date. Keep in the fridge for 2 days. The tea can be infused twice.

Add all the ingredients together to a chilled highball glass with ice cubes and give it a quick stir. Garnish with flowers.

From Stuart Bale of Strange Hill for the Bulgari Hotel, London.

HOOK, LINE, AND SINKER

30ml (1fl oz) West Winds Gin The Cutlass (*see* p.135)

40ml (1⅓fl oz) Regal Rogue Rosso vermouth

2 dashes of Angostura Bitters

2 dashes of orange Curaçao

pickled black cherry, to garnish

Stir the ingredients together and strain into a chilled coupette glass. Garnish with a pickled black cherry.

From Tim Philips of Bulletin Place, Sydney.

OLD FRIEND (right)

One more from Jim Meehan of New York's PDT bar (see also pp.206 and 211), who explains: "A distant cousin of the classic Old Pal cocktail, this bright, sophisticated sour shares many of the attributes of a valued companion."

45ml (1½fl oz) London Dry Gin (*see* p.63)

25ml (⅘fl oz) pink grapefruit juice

15ml (½fl oz) Campari

1½ tsp St Germain elderflower liqueur

lemon twist, to garnish

Shake the ingredients with ice, then strain into a chilled coupe glass. Garnish with a lemon twist.

PASTIS IN A PEAR T (right)

50ml (1¾fl oz) Tanqueray London Dry Gin (*see* p.110)

5ml (⅙fl oz) pastis

½ fresh pear, peeled, cored, and roughly chopped

15ml (½fl oz) fresh lemon juice

10ml (⅓fl oz) simple syrup or gomme (*see* p.188)

star anise, to garnish

Shake all the ingredients over ice and serve in a chilled coupe glass. Garnish with a star anise.

From Barrie Wilson, global brand ambassador, Tanqueray gin.

VICTORIA CALLING

40ml (1⅓fl oz) Melbourne Gin Company (MGC) Dry Gin

15ml (½fl oz) Seppeltsfield Flora Fino (DP117) sherry

10ml (⅓fl oz) fresh lemon juice

10ml (⅓fl oz) sugar syrup or gomme (*see* p.188)

20ml (⅗fl oz) white grapefruit juice

strip of grapefruit peel, to garnish

Put all the ingredients into a cocktail shaker, shake, and strain into a chilled coupette glass. Garnish with a strip of grapefruit peel.

From Tim Philips of Bulletin Place, Sydney.

PATCHOULI FIZZ (right)

40ml (1⅓fl oz) Beefeater London Garden Exclusive Edition gin

20ml (⅗fl oz) fresh lemon juice

5ml (⅙fl oz) Merlet Lune d'Abricot (apricot brandy)

10ml (⅓fl oz) simple syrup or gomme (*see* p.188)

10ml (⅓fl oz) green tea

2 dashes of patchouli bitters

Fever-Tree tonic water, to top up

FOR THE GARNISH

lemon wheel

micro basil

Add all ingredients, bar the tonic, to a cocktail shaker and shake over ice cubes. Fine strain into a chilled highball glass and top up with tonic. Garnish with a lemon wheel and micro basil.

From Nathan O'Neill, Dandelyan, Mondrian Hotel, London.

KUKU COOLER

8 seedless black grapes, plus extra to garnish

40ml (1⅓fl oz) Tanqueray London Dry Gin (*see* p.110)

15ml (½fl oz) Madeira wine

15ml (½fl oz) fresh lime luice

10ml (⅓fl oz) verjus (verjuice)

50ml (1¾fl oz) tonic water, to top up

lime wheel, to garnish

Muddle the grapes in a cocktail shaker, then add the rest of the ingredients, bar the tonic, and shake. Strain into a chilled highball glass and top up with the tonic. Garnish with a lime wheel and split black grapes.

From Matt Linklater, Bulletin Place, Sydney.

BIBLIOGRAPHY

Anderson, Frank J. *An Illustrated History of the Herbals*. New York: Columbia University Press, 1997.

Anon. *A Dissertation on Mr Hogarth's Six Prints*. London: 1751.

Anon. *Mother Gin: A Tragi-Comical Eclogue*. London: Homer's Head, 1737. Reprinted British Library Historical Print Collections, 2011.

Baker Jr, Charles H. *Jigger, Beaker, & Glass*. Lanham, Maryland: Derrydale Press, 1992.

Barnett, Richard. *The Book of Gin*. New York: Grove Press, 2011.

Bayley, Stephen. *Gin*. Norwich: Balding & Mansell, 1994.

Beekman, E M. *Fugitive Dreams*. Amherst: The University of Massachusetts Press, 1988.

Bennett, Thea. *London Gin*. Newhaven: Golden Guides Press, 2013.

Boothby, William. *The World's Drinks and How to Mix Them*. San Francisco: 1908. Reprinted Mud Puddle Books, 2009.

Brunschwig, Hieronymus. *Liber de Arte Distillandi de Compositis*. Strasbourg: 1512. National Library of Medicine ebook.

Cademan, Thomas. *The Distiller of London*. London: Sarah Paske, 1698. Reprinted Early English Books Online (EEBO) Editions, 2011.

Cooper, Ambrose. *The Complete Distiller*. London: P Vaillant and R Griffiths, 1757. Reprinted Kessinger Publishing, 2010.

Craddock, Harry. *The Savoy Cocktail Book*. London: Constable & Company, 1930.

Curtis, Tony & Williams, David G. *An Introduction to Perfumery*, second edition. New York: Micelle Press, 2001.

DeGroff, Dale. *The Craft of the Cocktail*. London: Proof Publishing, 2003.

Dickens, Cedric. *Drinking with Dickens*. New York: New Amsterdam Books, 1980.

Dickens, Charles. *Sketches by Boz*. London: 1839. Reprinted The Penguin Group, 1995.

Difford, Simon. *Diffordsguide Gin Compendium*, second edition. London: Old Firm of Sin, 2013.

Doxat, John. *The Gin Book*. London: Quiller Press Ltd, 1989.

Duffy, Patrick Gavin & Misch, Robert J. *The Official Mixer's Manual*. New York: R Long and R R Smith, 1934. Reprinted Doubleday, 1983.

Edmunds, Lowell. *Martini, Straight Up*. Baltimore: The Johns Hopkins University Press, 1998.

Embury, David A. *The Fine Art of Mixing Drinks*, revised edition. New York: Doubleday & Company, 1958.

English, George. "Flemish Religious Emigration in the 16th and 17th Centuries". *Scotland and the Flemish People*, University of St Andrews, 2014.

Fouquet, Louis. *Bariana*. Paris: 1896. Reprinted Mixellany, 2008.

George, Dorothy. *London Life in the Eighteenth Century*. London: Kegan Paul, Trench, Trubner and Co, 1925. Reprinted The Penguin Group, 1992.

Gesner, Conrad. *Historiae Animalium*. Zurich: 1551–8. National Library of Medicine ebook.

Grimes, William. *Straight Up or On the Rocks*. New York: North Point Press, 2001.

Gronow, Captain Rees Howell. *Reminiscences of Captain Gronow*. London: Smith, Elder, & Co, 1862. Project Gutenberg ebook.

Gwynn, Robin D. "England's 'First Refugees'". *History Today*, Vol 35, May 1985.

Haigh, Ted. *Vintage Spirits and Forgotten Cocktails*. Beverly, Massachusetts: Quarry Books, 2009.

Johnson, Harry. *The New and Improved Illustrated Bartenders' Manual*. New York: 1888. Reprinted Mixellany, 2009.

Knoll, Aaron J & Smith, David T. *The Craft of Gin*. Hayward: White Mule Press, 2013.

Lans, Nathalie. *Schiedam Builds on Jenever History*. Schiedam: TDS Drukwerken, 2000.

Loftus, William. *The New Mixing Book*. London: 1869. Reprinted Ross Bolton, 2008.

McHarry, Samuel. *The Practical Distiller*. Harrisburg: John Wyeth, 1809. Internet Archive.

Medwin, Thomas. *Conversations of Lord Byron*. London: 1824. Google Books.

Miller, Anistatia R & Brown, Jared M. *Shaken Not Stirred*. New York: HarperCollins, 1997.

Miller, Anistatia R & Brown, Jared M. *Spiritous Journey: A History of Drink, Book One*. London: Mixellany, 2009.

Miller, Anistatia R & Brown, Jared M. *Spiritous Journey: A History of Drink, Book Two*. London: Mixellany, 2009.

Miller, Anistatia R & Brown, Jared M. *The Mixellany Guide to Vermouth & Other Apéritifs*. Cheltenham: Mixellany, 2011.

Miller, John. "Portrait of Britain: 1600". *History Today*, Vol 50, September 2000.

Milton, Giles. *Nathaniel's Nutmeg*. London: Hodder & Stoughton, 1999.

Moran, Bruce T. *Distilling Knowledge: Alchemy, Chemistry, and the Scientific Revolution*. Cambridge, Massachusetts: Harvard University Press, 2005.

Morewood, Samuel. *A Philosophical and Statistical History of the Inventions and Customs of Ancient and Modern Nations in the Manufacture and Use of Inebriating Liquors*. Dublin: W Curry and W Carson, 1838. Reprinted Kessinger Publishing, 2012.

Parkinson, John. *Theatrum Botanicum: The Theater of Plants*. London: 1640. Google Books.

Plat, Hugh. *Delightes for Ladies*. London: 1609. Celtnet.

Regan, Gary. *The Joy of Mixology*. New York: Clarkson Potter Publishers, 2003.

Regan, Gaz. *The Negroni*. Cheltenham: Mixellany, 2012.

Ricket, E & Thomas, C. *The Gentleman's Table Guide*. London: 1871. Internet Archive.

Rocco, Fiammetta. *The Miraculous Fever-Tree*. London: HarperCollins, 2004.

Schmidt, William (The Only William). *The Flowing Bowl: What and When to Drink*. New York: Charles L Webster & Co, 1892.

Schumann, Charles. *American Bar*. New York: Abbeville Press Publishers, 1995.

Sell, Charles S. *The Chemistry of Fragrances*. Cambridge: Royal Society of Chemistry, 2006.

Solmonson, Lesley Jacobs. *Gin: A Global History*. London: Reaktion Books, 2012.

Stephen, John, MD. *A Treatise on the Manufacture, Imitation, Adulteration, and Reduction of Foreign Wines, Brandies, Gins, Rums, Etc*. Philadelphia: 1860. The Online Books Page.

Stewart, Amy. *The Drunken Botanist*. Chapel Hill, North Carolina: Algonquin Books, 2013.

Stiles, Henry Reed. *A History of the City of Brooklyn*. Brooklyn: 1869.

Stuart, Thomas. *Stuart's Fancy Drinks and How to Mix Them*. New York: Excelsior Publishing House, 1896. Internet Archive.

Terrington, William. *Cooling Cups and Dainty Drinks*. London and New York: Routledge and Sons, 1869. Internet Archive.

Thomas, Jerry. *The Bar-Tender's Guide*. New York: Dick & Fitzgerald, 1876. Reprinted Angouleme, Vintagebook, 2001.

Tudge, Colin. *The Secret Life of Trees*. London: The Penguin Group, 2005.

Van Acker, Veronique. *Genever: 500 Years of History in a Bottle*. Vermont: Flemish Lion, 2013.

Van Schoonenberghe, Eric. "Genever (Gin): A Spirit Drink Full of History, Science, and Technology". Ghent: *Sartoniana*, Vol 12, 1999.

Warner, Jessica. *Craze: Gin and Debauchery in an Age of Reason*. London: Profile Books, 2003.

Warner, Jessica. "The Naturalization of Beer and Gin in Early Modern England". *Contemporary Drug Problems*, Vol 24, Issue 2, 1997. Questia Trusted Online Research.

Williams, David G. *The Chemistry of Essential Oils*, second edition. Weymouth: Micelle Press, 2008.

Williams, Olivia. *Gin Glorious Gin*. London: Headline Publishing Group, 2014.

Wilson, Anne C. *Water of Life*. Devon: Prospect Books, 2006.

Wondrich, David. *Imbibe*! New York: The Penguin Group, 2007.

Wondrich, David. *Punch*. New York: The Penguin Group, 2010.

Y-Worth, W. *The Compleat Distiller*. London: J Taylor, 1705. Reprinted Gale Eighteenth Century Collections Online (ECCO), Print Editions, 2010.

Recipe titles for cocktails and mixers are in *italics*.
Page numbers for illustrations are in *italics*.

THANKS

PICTURE CREDITS

The publishers would like to thank all the distillers and their agents who have kindly provided images of their gins for inclusion in this book.

Additional credits are as follows:

Alamy Anton Havelaar 24; Bon Appetit 38; Falkenstein/Bildagentur-online Historical Collect 23; Jean-Baptiste Rabouan/Hemis 31; Jeffrey Blackler 33; Mary Evans Picture Library 21; Museum of London/ Heritage Image Partnership Ltd 18; Peter Horree 13; Tom Hanley 37; courtesy **Caorunn Gin** 43; **Corbis** David J Frent/David J & Janice L Frent Collection 26; courtesy of **Dave Broom** 11; **Getty Images** Brad Wenner 2; Chris Ratcliffe/ Bloomberg via Getty Images 34; Florilegius/SSPL 9; Guildhall Library & Art Gallery/Heritage Images 19; Imagno 15; Topical Press Agency 27, 29; courtesy **The Hendrick's Gin Distillery Ltd** 32, 42; courtesy **Lucas Bols** bv 12; courtesy **NY Distilling Company** 30; **Shutterstock** Nicku 25; S1001 36; SidorovichV 35; **Sipsmith Independent Spirits** photo Alastair Wiper 41; **Thinkstock** iStock 55; **Wellcome Library**, London 8, 10, 16; **Zuidam Distillers** bv 44, 45.

Author photo, page 7, by **Will Robb.**

Cocktails photographed by **Cristian Barnett** for Octopus Publishing.

This book has been long in gestation and could not have been written without the help, input, friendship, broad shoulders, and thirsty palates of many colleagues, friends, and family members.

To Desmond Payne, who showed me the way of gin all those years ago and who has been a constant source of help - and gin - ever since.

To Sean Harrison for Tales memories, help on chemistry, lunch on a train, and more.

To Patrick Zuidam, who is taking genever into a new world.

To Jean-Sébastien Robicquet, Jamie Walker, and the team at G'Vine.

To Will Lowe for crafting me my own gin, organoleptic advice, and ants.

To Alexandre Gabriel, Alex Nicol, Darren Rook, Simon Ford, Charles Maxwell, Jake Burger, and all who sent samples.

To Anistatia Miller for always being a sounding board, and Jared Brown for the same, along with Sam and Fairfax for some great juniper-laden memories.

To Geoffrey Kelly for Flemish gin, Neil Mathieson for the "boutique" tasting, and Michael Vachon for the same.

To Nicholas Cook at the Gin Guild, and the staff at the Schiedam Museum.

To Charles Rolls for piloting me safely so many years ago, and his colleagues Tim Warrillow and Saskia Meyer at Fever-Tree.

To Joanne McKerchar at Diageo Archive for immense help with historical detail.

To David T Smith at summerfruitcup.wordpress.com for ears and laying on a great tasting.

To Sandrae Lawrence and Gary Sharpen, Gin Cocktail lovers and dear friends.

To Ryan Chetiyawardana for once again doing the cocktail shoot despite huge work pressures, and to Tristan Stephenson and the team at Whistling Shop for allowing us to use their great bar, Barrie Wilson, the second-best bartender in Dunfermline, Tony C, Tim D Philips, Naren Young, Jim Meehan, Stu Bale, the Lyan Group barkeeps, Nick Strangeway and Cairbry Hill, Dick Bradsell, and Seb Hamilton-Mudge.

To Philip Duff for all his help on genever, Gaz Regan for his finger, and David Wondrich for advice administered in various Canadian dive bars - truly a sage who knows his onions.

To the members of the SKYC, for whom three Negronis is never enough.

To the Octopus team, who once again have done a magnificent job: Denise, Leanne, Giulia, Juliette, and Jo the editor.

To Tom Williams, my patient, helpful, and unflappable agent - and fellow Negroni fiend.

Mostly, however, to my wife Jo, who not only has supported me during the writing but has been a partner in the process. Without her handling of research and logistics, this book wouldn't be here, or I'd be mad... or both. At least at the end of this she now realizes that she likes cocktails, which, in another serendipitous occurrence, can now be shaken like the devil by our daughter Rosie, who may be too young to drink but can make a killer Aviation. Long may you fly.